HOUSING
OF THE
ELDERLY
IN IRELAND

THE N

First published 1985
by the National Council for the Aged
Corrigan House, Fenian Street, Dublin 2
and distributed by The Glendale Press Ltd.,
45 Patrick Street, Dun Laoghaire,
Co. Dublin.

Cover design by Declan Buckley

ORIGINATION BY
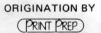

TABLE OF CONTENTS

5

Task Force on Special Housing Aid for the Elderly
Elderly Owner Occupiers
Caring for the Elderly at Home
Co-ordination of Services for the Elderly at Local Level
Health and Housing Authorities

APPENDICES

Appendix 1
Tables relating to Demographic Considerations.

Appendix 2
Population Projections by County and Planning Region, 1981–2006 (Prepared for the National Council for the Aged by John Blackwell).

Appendix 3
Projections of Number of Elderly Persons Living Alone, 1981–2006 (Prepared for the National Council for the Aged by John Blackwell).

Appendix 4
Exceptional Compassionate Grounds for Allocation of Housing Points by Dublin Corporation.

Appendix 5
Diagrammatic Representation of Community Context for Sheltered Housing Schemes.

Appendix 6
Legislation relevant to Voluntary Housing Associations.

Appendix 7
Legal Incorporation for Voluntary Housing Associations.

Appendix 8
The Guiding Principles of the Abbeyfield Society.

Appendix 9
Leasehold Schemes for the Elderly in Great Britain.

Appendix 10
Fire Safety for the Elderly at Home.

LIST OF TABLES

ACKNOWLEDGEMENTS

The members of the present National Council for the Aged would like to pay special tribute to their predecessors on the last Council who laid the foundation for this report in initial drafts.

It wishes to thank Mr. John Carroll, of the Department of the Environment, and Mr. Michael Kelly and Mr. Frank Goodwin, of the Welfare Section of Dublin Corporation, for their particular assistance and advice. Voluntary organisations, particularly Threshold Ltd. and the Housing Centre, were also most helpful in contributing detailed and relevant information.

The very useful detailed projections contained in Appendices 2 and 3 are the work of Mr. John Blackwell who has thereby made a most valuable contribution to this report.

On the 13th and 14th June, 1985 the Council organised a consultative seminar on Housing and Institutional Care of the Elderly at which participants responded to a draft of this report and of the report *Institutional Care of the Elderly in Ireland,* which is being published simultaneously. We wish to thank all those who attended for sharing their experience of care of the elderly with us. But most particularly we are indebted to Mr. B. Desmond T.D., Minister for Health and Social Welfare, Dr. D.H. Dick, Consultant Psychiatrist and former Director of the Health Advisory Service (Britain), Mr. P. Morrisey, Housing Coordinator and Assistant City Manager (Dublin) and Mr. D. O'Shea, Chief Executive Officer, North Western Health Board, for their stimulating addresses to this seminar.

We are particularly grateful to our small staff, Mr. Bob Carroll, Mr. Michael Browne and Ms. Jennifer Leech, for their industry in the research, writing, production and typing of this report.

L.J. Tuomey
Chairman.

INTRODUCTION

This report on *Housing of the Elderly in Ireland* is a companion volume to the report *Institutional Care of the Elderly in Ireland* and the two should be read in conjunction with one another. Previous reports published by the National Council for the Aged, notably *Day Hospital Care, Community Services for the Elderly* and *Home from Home?* are also related to the present report, as are forthcoming studies by the Council on Transport, on Private and are forthcoming studies by the Council on Transport, on Private and Voluntary Nursing Homes and on Family Carers.

The report has a number of underlying criteria which can be stated as follows:

(a) The desire to retain independence and/or to remain living in the community should be respected at all times. People should be helped and encouraged to live in their own homes and in their own communities for as long as they wish and are able to do so.

(b) Elderly people should be, at all times, given the facilities and opportunities to function independently and to retain their identity as individual persons. There are powerful social arguments against institutionalising elderly persons.

(c) Adequate and suitable living accommodation is even more important for the elderly than for the rest of society because in many instances their abodes are the centre of all their activities. Housing for the elderly must thus be viewed as more than mere shelter. Its psychological and social significance should not be underestimated. Housing policies should be aimed at enabling the aged to live, if they wish, in locations that are familiar to them, where their involvement in the community may be of long standing and where they will have the opportunity to live a rich and normal life with a maximum degree of independence and security. To achieve this aim, housing policies should operate with sensitivity and flexibility and in tandem with other social policies both at national and local level.

11

(d) The needs of the aged in any area should be looked at as a whole and dealt with locally in a flexible manner. This necessitates a wide range of provision, from community care services for elderly persons living at home to long-stay extended nursing care units for those who require such care. Such a provision should include day care facilities, day hospital facilities, sheltered housing provision, respite and intermittent care facilities and in-patient hospital facilities.

(e) There is an inter-relationship between the need for community support services, such as house repairs, special housing, sheltered housing, welfare accommodation, day hospitals, in-patient facilities and the respective scale of provision of any of these services or facilities. A deficiency in one is very likely to manifest itself in an increased demand for another. Thus an integrated and co-ordinated approach by the health boards and the housing authorities is considered essential.

(f) Absolute and continuing increases in the numbers of people who are living into old age, coupled with increased social mobility and diminishing family size, has led to a situation where there is a greater need for state intervention in all areas relating to the welfare of the aged. Housing policy is an important and an integral part of this intervention.

The Council recognises that inadequate housing has frequently resulted in an elderly person being unnecessarily admitted to hospital or to long-term institutional care. The provision of adequate and appropriate housing will enable many more elderly people to be cared for at home by the community care network — family, voluntary and statutory. It will postpone and may even obviate the need for institutional care.

It is now necessary to review the adequacy of the current network of family and community support systems for the elderly with a view to providing the level of support required to anable elderly persons to live independently in the community for the maximum period of time. The type, structure, location, facilities and support services of housing provided are fundamental in this respect. The Council sees the provision of a broad range of housing options for the elderly as they key to lessening the need for hospital and institutional care.

Thus, greater consideration should be given to the needs of the elderly within the overall housing programme. There is also a need for a more effective co-ordination of services for the elderly currently separately provided by the Departments of the Environment and Health at national level and by local authorities and health boards at regional and county level.

Many of the recommendations contained in this report are likely to

12

require greater financial resources in order to cater for the wide range of housing options and related services for elderly persons that are put forward. The shift in emphasis away from institutional care to community-based care has at times been based on the widely held belief that community care represents a cheaper alternative, a very significant factor when governments are looking to cut public expenditure. However, the Council wishes to emphasise that the relative costs of community and institutional care are very difficult to establish. It may well be that the full costs of adequate and appropriate housing for elderly persons coupled with the necessary level of domiciliary and support services are not far removed from those of institutional care.

This report identifies many areas where further research is required before the housing needs of the elderly can be comprehensively established and provided for. It is to be hoped that such research will be carried out during the coming years, not only at national level where this is appropriate, but also at regional and local level. In this respect the Central Policy Review Staff in Britain stated

"where allocation of resources at a regional or sub-regional level is involved ... changes in population in the country as a whole are often less important than local needs and demands which are themselves likely to have been influenced by changes in the distribution of population and in the patterns of internal migration".[1]

The various housing options for elderly persons identified throughout this report should be viewed as complementary strategies in a field where totally ideal solutions are unlikely to be attainable. People in later life do not form a homogenous group. Their circumstances are as diverse as the rest of the population, as are their housing needs. The range of housing options available should reflect the individuality and diversity of these housing needs and should ensure that the elderly continue as active participants in the community and so avoid becoming marginalised, isolated and dependent.

The National Council for the Aged
Corrigan House
Fenian Street
Dublin 2.

At time of going to print, the Housing (Miscellaneous Provisions) Bill, 1985 was published. The bill refers to a number of areas discussed in this report. It has not been possible to include discussion of either provisions of this bill in the present report or of the 1985 House Improvement Grant Scheme due to take effect from 1st December 1985.

CHAPTER 1

DEMOGRAPHIC CONSIDERATIONS

The Elderly Population

In 1981, there were some 369,000 elderly persons (i.e. those aged 65 years and over) in Ireland, representing 10.7% of the total population. In the decade between 1971 and 1981 there was an increase of 12% in the elderly population but a very slight decline in the proportion of elderly persons in the total population. Those aged 75 years and over represent 4% of the entire population and 36% of all elderly persons in the population. Those aged 80 years and over represent less than 2% of the entire population and just over 17% of all elderly persons (see Table 1.1).

TAKE IN TABLE 1.1

Table 1.1: *Population Aged 65 Years and Over by Age-Group –*
in Parenthesis is Proportion of Total Population

Age Group	1966	1971	1981	% change 1966-71	% change 1971-81
65 and over	323,007 (11.2)	329,819 (11.1)	368,954 (10.7)	2.1	11.9
75 and over	118,682 (4.1)	119,082 (4.0)	131,897 (3.8)	0.3	10.8
80 and over	55,881 (1.9)	57,307 (1.9)	63,446 (1.8)	2.6	10.7

Source: *Census of Population, 1981,* Volume 2
Central Statistics Office, Dublin.

The proportion of elderly people in Ireland in 1982 relative to the total population was lower than in any other EEC country and considerably lower than in Great Britain, where the elderly comprise 15% of the total population (See Table 1.2).

In 1981 women accounted for 55% of all elderly persons and for 60% of those aged 75 years and over and for 63% of those aged 80 years and over. These figures reflect the greater longevity of women's lives. [1]

15

Table 1.2: *Total Population and Percentage distribution by age for EEC Countries, 1982*

Country	Total Population '000	Percentage aged			
		0-14 years	15-44 years	46-64 years	65 years and over
Belgium	9,856.3	19.7	43.3	23.3	13.8
Denmark	5.117.8	19.7	44.4	21.2	14.7
France	54,218.6	21.9	43.2	21.6	13.4
German Federal Republic	61,637.6	16.9	44.8	23.3	15.1
Greece	9,392.0	22.2	40.9	23.6	13.3
Ireland	3,483.0	30.3	42.2	16.9	10.6
Italy	57,195.5	21.4	42.4	22.6	13.6
Luxembourg	365.5	18.2	45.2	23.1	13.5
Netherlands	14,312.6	21.2	47.1	19.9	11.7
United Kingdom	56,340.7	20.2	42.7	22.1	15.0

Source: *Statistical Information Relevant to the Health Services,* Department of Health, 1984, Table A5.

In Ireland there is a tendency for the elderly to be more heavily represented in the rural than in the urban population, a tendency which is quite marked in some of the western counties, particularly in Leitrim, Mayo and Roscommon. (See Table 1.3). Here the percentages of the total area population who are elderly are significantly higher than the percentages in some of the eastern counties — for example, 17.6% in Leitrim as compared with 9.8% in Carlow. A similar picture emerges when we look at the regional health board areas. (See Table 1.4). The percentage of the total population who were aged 65 years of age and over is much higher in the North Western and Western Health Board areas than in the Eastern Health Board area — 14.5% and 14.1% respectively as compared with 8.5%.

16

Table 1.3: *Percentage Distribution of Population in Age Groups*
for each County and County Borough, 1981.

County or County Borough	Age Group					
	0-14 years	15-24 years	25-44 years	45-64 years	65 years and over	"Dependent" Groups 0-14 years and 65 years and over
Carlow	32.4	17.5	23.4	16.9	9.8	42.3
Dublin Co. and Co. Borough	29.2	20.0	25.9	16.3	8.6	37.8
Dublin Co. Borough	*23.9*	*23.1*	*22.6*	*19.3*	*11.1*	*35.0*
Dun Laoghaire Borough	*24.0*	*20.0*	*22.6*	*19.5*	*13.8*	*37.9*
Dublin*	*36.6*	*16.1*	*30.5*	*12.1*	*4.7*	*41.3*
Kildare	34.5	16.9	28.1	13.6	6.9	41.4
Kilkenny	30.9	16.4	24.1	17.7	10.9	41.8
Loaighis	31.5	16 8	22.8	18.0	11.0	42.5
Longford	30.1	15.6	22.4	19.2	12.7	42.8
Louth	32.0	17.5	24.7	16.6	9.2	41.2
Meath	34.0	16.2	25.8	15.3	8.7	42.7
Offaly	32.2	17.3	22.4	17.9	10.2	42.4
Westmeath	31.4	17.3	23.3	17.7	10.4	41.8
Wexford	32.0	16.2	23.4	17.0	11.3	43.3
Wicklow	32.4	16.0	26.3	15.7	9.6	41.9
Clare	30.8	14.7	24.4	17.6	12.5	43.3
Cork Co. and Co. Borough	30.0	17.3	24.2	17.4	11.1	41.1
Cork Co. Borough	*28.4*	*21.1*	*22.9*	*17.6*	*10.0*	*38.4*
Cork	*30.9*	*15.4*	*24.8*	*17.3*	*11.6*	*42.5*
Kerry	29.0	15.4	22.9	18.7	14.0	43.0
Limerick Co and Co Borough	30.8	17.7	24.3	17.1	10.1	41.0
Limerick Co. Borough	*30.0*	*20.9*	*23.1*	*16.9*	*9.1*	*39.1*
Limerick	*31.3*	*15.8*	*24.9*	*17.2*	*10.7*	*42.1*
Tipperary N.R.	30.6	16.3	22.5	18.8	11.9	42.4
Tipperary S.R.	30.8	17.1	22.6	18.3	11.3	42.1
Waterford Co. and Co. Borough	31.2	17.0	24.1	17.3	10.4	41.6
Waterford Co. Borough	*31.2*	*18.8*	*24.7*	*16.3*	*9.0*	*40.3*
Waterford	*31.1*	*15.6*	*23.7*	*18.0*	*11.5*	*42.7*
Galway	29.8	17.2	23.3	17.2	12.5	42.3
Leitrim	26.1	14.4	20.9	21.0	17.6	43.7
Mayo	28.8	14.9	21.4	19.0	15.9	44.7
Roscommon	28.2	14.7	20.7	20.7	15.6	43.9
Sligo	28.2	15.8	22.9	18.8	14.2	42.5
Cavan	28.8	15.7	21.6	20.2	13.8	42.5
Donegal	31.3	15.1	22.5	17.2	14.0	45.2
Monaghan	30.4	16 1	22.9	18.3	12.3	42.7

*Excluding Dun Laoghaire Borough

Source: *Census of Population, 1981,* Volume 2,
Central Statistics Office, Dublin.

Table 1.4: *Population of each Health Board Area by Age and by Sex, 1981*

		Eastern	Midland	Mid-Western	North-Eastern	North-Western	South-Eastern	Southern	Western	Ireland
Total population:		1,194,735	202,146	308,212	288,980	208,195	374,575	525,235	341,327	3,443,405
Age Groups:										
	0-14 years	357,581	63,554	94,896	91,871	61,968	117,578	156,516	99,765	1,043,729
Number	15-44 years	544,158	80,208	124,970	117,470	78,158	150,879	213,843	130,634	1,440,320
	45-64 years	191,426	36,478	54,085	49,505	37,822	65,331	93,162	62,593	590,402
	65-74 years	65,437	13,903	22,100	19,538	19,185	25,961	40,081	30,852	237,057
	75 years and over	36,133	8,003	12,161	10,596	11,062	14,826	21,633	17,483	131,897
	0-14 years	29.9	31.4	30.8	31.8	29.8	31.4	29.8	29.2	30.3
Percentage	15-44 years	45.5	39.7	40.5	40.6	37.5	40.3	40.7	38.3	41.8
	45-64 years	16.0	18.0	17.5	17.1	18.2	17.4	17.7	18.3	17.1
	65-74 years	5.5	6.9	7.2	6.8	9.2	6.9	7.6	9.0	6.9
	75 years and over	3.0	4.0	3.9	3.7	5.3	4.0	4.1	5.1	3.8
Marital status (persons aged 15 years and over)										
	Single	326,217	54,006	81,511	73,878	58,217	97,176	143,093	97,850	931,948
Number	Married	455,932	73,901	115,256	108,435	75,462	139,650	196,299	123,165	1,288,100
	Widowed	55,005	10,685	16,549	14,796	12,548	20,171	29,327	20,547	179,628
	Single	39.0	39.0	38.2	37.5	39.8	37.8	38.8	40.5	38.8
Percentage	Married	54.5	53.3	54.0	55.0	51.6	54.3	53.2	51.0	53.7
	Widowed	6.6	7.7	7.8	7.5	8.6	7.8	8.0	8.5	7.5
Dependency ratio (number of persons aged 0-14 years and aged 65 years or over as a percentage of those aged 15- 64 years)		62.4	73.2	72.1	73.1	79.5	73.2	71.1	76.6	69.6

Source: *Statistical Information Relevant to the Health Services,* Department of Health, 1984.

Improvements in social and economic conditions have led to a significant improvement in life expectation, particularly for women at various ages over the past thirty years, as can be seen from Table 1.5

Table 1.5: *Life Expectancy. Expectation of Life at selected ages from 1950 to 1980*

		Period			
		1950-52	1960-62	1970-72	1978-80
Males: Number of additional years a person can expect to live at age	0	64.5	68.1	68.8	69.5
	1	66.9	69.3	69.2	69.5
	5	63.6	65.7	65.5	65.7
	25	44.8	46.4	46.3	46.4
	45	27.0	27.8	27.6	27.7
	65	12.1	12.6	12.4	12.4
	75	6.8	7.1	7.3	7.1
Females: Number of additional years a person can expect to live at at age	0	67.1	71.9	73.5	75.0
	1	68.8	72.7	73.8	74.8
	5	65.4	69.0	70.0	71.0
	25	46.6	49.5	50.5	51.4
	45	28.9	30.7	31.4	32.1
	65	13.3	14.4	15.0	15.4
	75	7.6	8.1	8.5	8.8

Source: *Statistical Information Relevant to the Health Services.* Department of Health, 1984, Table A6.

It should be noted, however, that there has been very little increase in life expectancy for men in older age-groups in the period 1950-1980. Furthermore, the life expectancy at 65 years for all persons in Ireland is lower than in all other EEC countries with the exception of Luxembourg (Appendix 1, Table 3).

Marital Status
In 1981 the breakdown of the elderly population according to marital status was as follows: (see also Appendix 1, Table 4)

	Aged 65 and Over	Aged 75 and Over
Single	25%	25%
Married	42%	28%
Widowed	34%	47%

Almost 50% of women aged 65 years and over and 60% of women aged 75 years and over are widows and in each case outnumber widowers by more than three to one. This is due, not only to the greater longevity of women's lives, but also because married women tend to be younger than their husbands.

Elderly Households [2]
In 1981 the number of private households where the head of the household was aged 65 and over was 206,800. This represented a 14% increase in the number of households since 1971. Table 1.6 indicates that the proportion of persons aged 65 years and over living alone or in man and wife households has increased significantly while those living in other types of private households has declined.

In the twenty year period between 1961 and 1981 the population of elderly persons living alone or in man and wife households increased from 19.7% to 36.7%. However, despite these increases, it should be noted that a sizeable proportion of elderly persons continue to live in other types of private households (55% in 1981).

In Ireland, as in a number of other countries, the tendancy has been for an increasing number of elderly persons to live in separate households, as distinct from living in households together with adult sons and daughters, or with relatives. This tendency reflects the social and economic changes brought about by factors such as an increased desire for independence and a greater ability to attain it (both on the part of the elderly and on the part of their families), increased urbanisation and some increase in labour mobility which necessitates people living at a distance from their elderly relatives.

In 1981 there was 68,000 elderly persons living alone in Ireland. [3] This represented 18.4% of elderly persons and a 57% increase on 1971 figures. In

20

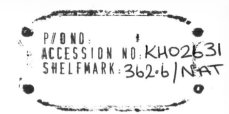

Table 1.6: *Eldery Persons Classified by Type of Household, 1961, 1966, 1971, 1979, 1981*

Type of Household	1961		1966		1971		1979		1981	
	Number	%	Number	%	Number	%	Number	%	Number	%
One Person	32,210	10.2	35,024	10.8	43,378	13.1	61,327	17.0	68,034	18.4
Man and Wife	30,058	9.5	35,977	11.1	44,754	13.6	62,685	17.3	67,364	18:3
Mult-Member Total	228,550	72.6	225,640	69.9	214,820	65.1	208,425	57.7	202,961	55.0
Man and wife and one or more children (of any age)							46,594	12.9	45,131	12.2
Man or wife with other persons							15,239	4.2	15,507	4.2
Man and wife and one or more children (of any age) with other persons							39,875	11.0	39,530	10.7
Lone parent and one or more children (of any age) with or without other persons							40,186	11.1	39,801	10.8
Other							66,531	18.5	62,922	17.1
Non-Private Houshlods[1]	24,245	7.7	26,366	8.2	27,136	8.2	28,938	8.0	30,595	8.3
All Types	315,063	100.0	323,007	100.0	329,819	100.0	361,375	100.0	368,954	100.0

[1] A non-private household is a boarding house, hotel, guesthouse, barrack, hospital, nursing home, boarding school, religious institution, welfare institution, prison or ship.

Source: *Census of Population 1961, Census of Population 1966, Census of Population 1971, Census of Population 1979, Census of Population 1981,* Central Statistics Office, Dublin 2.

21

this category of elderly persons living alone women outnumber men by almost 2:1.

Projection of Population Trends Among the Elderly [4]

In 2006 it is projected that there will be 396,500 persons aged 65 years and over in the country, representing 10.4% of the total population, of which 58% will be women.

Table 1.7 shows that in the period up to 2006 the elderly population itself is expected to age. From 1981 to 2006 there is expected to be a 20.2% increase in the number of elderly persons aged 75 years and over, by comparison with a 7.4% increase in the number aged 65 years and over and a 10.5% increase in the population as a whole.

Those aged 80 years and over numbered 63,400 in 1981 and constituted 17% of the elderly population. This figure is projected to rise to 81,200 in 2006 or to over 20% of the elderly population.

Regional Variations in Population Projections (See Appendix 1 Tables 5 and 6)

It is expected that the projected increases in the elderly population will not be distributed evenly throughout the country. While an overall national increase of 7.4% in the elderly population is expected during the period 1981-2006, some areas will experience actual decreases in both absolute and relative terms (e.g. Donegal, Kerry, Longford and all the counties of Connnaught) while other will experience substantial increases (e.g. Dublin County). In some instances the percentage of elderly in the total area population will increase even though there will be a decrease in the actual number of elderly persons in the area. For example, in Dublin County Borough the number of elderly persons is expected to decrease by over 9% in the period 1981-2006, but the actual percentage of elderly in the total area population will increase from 11% to 26%.

The number of those aged 75 years and over is expected to increase from 31,900 in 1981 to 158,500 in 2006, an increase of over 20%. The increase in this age-group for Counties Carlow, Kildare, Louth, Meath and Wicklow and for the County Boroughs of Limerick, Waterford and Cork is expected to be higher than the national average. In the case of Dublin County the number of those aged 75 years and over in the area is expected to more than double in the 25 year period. In the case of Leitrim and Roscommon there will be a decrease in the number aged 75 years and over.

Full details of these projections are given in Appendix 1 Tables 5 and 6 and in Appendix 2.

22

Table 1.7: *Population Projections for those aged 65 years and over,*
1981 – 2006

	1981	1986	1991	1996	2001	2006	% Change 1981-2006
			Males				
Over 65	165.2	167.5	167.3	164.7	163.2	167.4	(1.3)
Over 75	52.5	55.8	58.9	58.7	57.8	56.7	(8.0)
Over 80	23.3	23.3	25.1	26.4	26.0	25.6	(9.9)
All Ages	1729.5	1797.9	1832.4	1851.4	1859.5	1903.2	(10.1)
			Females				
Over 65	203.8	213.3	220.6	222.2	222.6	229.1	(12.4)
Over 75	79.4	84.3	91.5	95.7	99.9	101.9	(28 3)
Over 80	40.1	41.8	44.5	49.2	52.0	55.6	(38.6)
All Ages	1714.0	1786.3	1823.6	1845.0	1855.0	1907.7	(10.9)
			Persons				
Over 65	369.0	381.0	387.9	387.0	385.9	396.5	(7.4)
Over 75	131.9	140.1	150.4	154.5	157.8	158.6	(20.2)
Over 80	63.4	65.1	69.6	75.6	78.1	81.2	(28.1)
All Ages	3443.4	3584.2	3656.0	3696.4	3714.5	3804.9	(10.5)

Source: *Appendix 2*

Projection of Number of Elderly Persons Living Alone

During the period 1971-1981 there was a dramatic increase (57%) in the number of elderly persons living alone, from 43,400 in 1971 to 68,000 in 1981.

In 1981 there were 24,100 elderly male persons living alone. It is projected that in 2006 there will be 21,500 such persons, representing an 11% decrease over the 25 year period.

In 1981 there were 44,000 elderly female persons living alone. It is projected that in 2006 there will be 67,900 such persons, representing a 54% increase over the period.

These figures show a projected overall growth of 31% in the number of elderly persons living alone in the period up to 2006. (See Appendix 3 for a fuller discussion of this topic).

CHAPTER 2

HOUSING CIRCUMSTANCES OF THE ELDERLY

Introduction

Housing need has been defined as the extent to which the quantity and quality of existing accommodation falls short of that required to provide each household or person in the population, irrespective of ability to pay or of particular personal preferences, with accommodation of a specified minimun standard and above. [1]

Housing policy in Ireland has frequently tended to emphasise the number of units built rather than the quality of the housing or the quality of the environment in which the housing is located. Housing quality and housing amenities are of particular importance for the elderly since the home is frequently the centre of virtually all of their activity. As people grow older the facilities, amenities and structure of their living accommodation should be such as to enhance rather than inhibit or stifle the quality of their lives. "Housing is a fundamental determinant of living conditions among elderly people and influences not only the ability of frail elderly people to care for themselves, but also helps determine the extent to which others can help support the elderly." [2] A recent enquiry [3], held in one county district, into the facilities and services which were thought to be most important to the elderly and disabled found that the provision of water and toilet facilities were regarded as the most important.

In Ireland, there are a number of differences between the housing circumstances of the elderly, when compared with those of the general population. The elderly are more likely to be owner occupiers. They are also likely to live in considerably older housing units which tend to be less well equipped with basic amenities than the housing of the general population. This position is not unique to Ireland. In England and Wales a survey, conducted in 1978, showed that half of the occupants of poor condition accommodation were elderly and retired. [4]

24

Housing Stock

There has been a significant improvement in the average level of Irish housing stock particularly in the last decade. The total housing stock increased by 23% between 1971 and 1981. During the period the total population increased by less than 16%. Table 2.1 gives an indication of the development during the ten year period.

It would appear from Table 2.1 that, between 1971 and 1981, some 50,000 to 60,000 pre-First World War dwellings became obsolete and had been replaced by more modern dwellings, reducing the number of pre-1919 built houses from 45% to under 30% of the total over the ten year period.

Housing Stock of the Elderly

However, as might be expected, the dwellings occupied by the elderly tend to be older than those occupied by younger people. An ESRI survey [5] carried out in 1977 showed that about 39% of the dwellings occupied by the elderly in urban areas were built before 1919 compared with 23% for the population as a whole. In rural areas the corresponding figures were 53% and 46%. Single person households, according to the ESRI report, tended to live in older dwellings than did other types of household. The St. Vincent de Paul survey [6] carried out in 1978 found that 53% of the old and alone lived in housing built prior to 1919. According to the 1981 Census of Population a total of 3,156 persons aged 65 and over lived in temporary housing units with 1,949 of those living alone. [7]

Housing Amenities

While factors other than the age and facilities of a dwellings can determine whether it is fit or unfit, the change in the age profile and the increases in the level of facilities available in the housing stock suggest a significant improvement in average housing conditions in recent years. It has been estimated that the level of unfitness in the housing stock has fallen from almost 12% in 1973 to about 8% in 1980. [8]

The increased modernisation of the housing stock is reflected in improvements in basic household amenities and, in particular, in sanitation facilities, as can be seen from Tables 2.2 and 2.3.

Between 1971 and 1980 the number of dwellings with a flush toilet increased from 71% to 90% of the total, with the result that in 1981 almost 93% of the population had access to a flush toilet. On the other hand the percentage of dwellings with no toilet or closet decreased from over 19% in 1971 to 7% in 1981.

In 1971 some 154,000 dwellings, or 21%, had no piped water supply while some 321,000, or 44% did not have the use of a fixed bath or shower. In

Table 2.1: *Dwellings (1981) and Housing Units 1971) Classified by Period in which Built*

Year	Before 1919	1919 to 1940	1941 to 1960	Period in which built 1961 to 1970	1971 to 1975	1976 or later	Not stated	Total
1971 (Housing Units)								
No. (000)	315.8	139.1	141.2	108.6			0.6	705.2*
Percentage	44.8	19.7	20.0	15.4			0.1	100.0
1981 (Dwellings)								
No. (000)	263.9	144.3	144.6	109.4	114.7	111.2	6.4	894.0
Percentage	29.5	16.1	16.2	12.2	12.8	12.4	0.7	100.0

*Covering 726,400 dwellings.
Source: *Census of Population, 1981. Fiver Per Cent Sample Estimates Housing and Households.* Central Statistics Office, Dublin.

Table 2.2: *Percentage of the Housing Stock with Selected Facilities 1971 and 1980 (estimated)*

	1971 %	1980 %
(a) Water Supply		
Internal	73.2	90.2
External	4.9	5.5
(b) Fixed bath or shower	55.4	80.5
(c) Sanitary facilities	70.0	88.9
(d) Electricity	94.7	98.9
(e) Central heating	N.A.	34.7

Source: *The Human Settlements Situation and Related Trends and Policies.* Department of the Envirionemnt Monograph, 1983.

Table 2.3: *Dwellings Classified by Sanitary Facilities, 1971 and 1981*

Year	Flush toilet	Chemical closet	Dry closet	No toilet or closet	Total (including not stated)
1971 No. (000)	514.5	17.1	54.6	140.2	726.4
Percentage	70.8	2.4	7.5	19.3	100.0
1981 No. (000)	801.3	8.5	19.2	61.6	894.4
Percentage	89.6	1.0	2.1	6.9	100.0

Source: *Census of Population, 1981 Five Per Cent Sample Estimates, Housing and Households.* Central Statistics Office, Dublin.

1981, the number of dwellings without piped water had declined to about 45,000, or 5%, while the number without a fixed bath or shower in 1981 was some 425,000, or 13%, of persons in private households in permanent housing units. [9]

Housing Amenities of the Elderly
The position of elderly households in respect of water and sanitation facilit-ies appears to be less favourable than that of the population as a whole. While

the data available on elderly households is not directly comparable with the data available on households in general, the figures of 31% of all elderly households with no inside WC and 38% with no bath or shower seem excessively high and indicate an unfavourable position of the elderly relative to the population as a whole (see Table 2.4).

Table 2.4: *Household Facilities of Elderly Households by Age of Head, 1980*

	Age of Head		Single Person Households by Age of Head	
	65 and over	80 and over	65 and over	80 and over
% of households with:				
Washing machine	34.8	22.4	13.2	12.0
Refrigerator	73.3	59.7	57.2	47.5
Television Set – col.	29.3	21.1	17.0	20.7
mono.	55.3	58.3	54.4	45.5
Piped water — cold	85.2	86.2	79.5	83.9
— hot	64.1	56.2	55.3	46.3
Bath of shower	62.3	52.1	53.0	46.6
Toilet (internal)	69.5	61.4	62.7	57.1
Telephone	24.1	21.8	23.3	26.1
Medical Card	77.4	86.2	80.7	89.2

Source: *Incomes of the Elderly in Ireland: and An Analysis of the States Contribution,* National Council for the Aged, 1984.

The position of elderly households whose head is aged oU years and over is less favourable in respect of water and sanitation facilities than other elderly households. 39% of such households do not have an internal toilet and 48% do not have a bath or shower.

Estimates from the 1981 Census of Population show 40% of all dwellings with central heating.[10] In urban areas in 1978, households headed by retired persons were almost three times less likely to have central heating than other urban households. [11]

In the ESRI survey 43% of elderly respondents complained of draughts while 33% cited dampness as a problem and for 9% traffic noise was stated to be a problem. [12]

While the Council does not have detailed information on the degree of fitness of elderly people's dwellings indications from various parts of the country are that a sizeable number of houses occupied by the elderly lack one or more basic amenities.

Martin and Doyle concluded, from a medico-social survey of the elderly in an urban general practice, that in many cases, "housing is sub-standard or unsuitable". [13] They found that 5% of the elderly attending a city centre practice had no indoor toilet or hot water. Kelleher and O'Mahony,[14] in a study of marginal farmers found that 26% of the houses occupied by those in the retired category (i.e. landowners who have retired or semi-retired from farming) were rated as being in a "poor" or "very poor" state of repair with 60% having neither hot water on tap nor a bathroom. Some 70% of this retired category were aged 71 years and over and 45.5% of them live alone. The authors conclude that "there were indicators of substantial deprivation among this category in terms of their standards of living and general life-style". [15]

A survey[16] of 60 selected people on the District Public Health Nurses "At risk" register, many of whom were elderly persons, carried out in 1984 in one area of a health board, reveals a serious lack of household amenities and facilities. Table 2.5 presents a selected summary of the findings.

Table 2.5: *Household Amenities of 60 Selected Persons On At Risk Register in One Health Board Area 1984*

	Have/Yes	Have Not/No
Electricity	33	27
Piped Water	13	31 (neither)
Piped Water Outside Only	16	
Suitable Toilet	8	52
Outside Light	14	46
Fuel Store	24	36

Source: Solan J., Paper presented at a conference,' *The Elderly in Rural Areas: Issue for Policy and Practice"* held at the National Institute for Higher Education, Limerick, December 1984.

The fact that "the district was not selected to be in any way unrepresentative — our nurses say it is fairly typical and would not be the worst" [17] indicates a sizeable problem in respect of housing accommodation and housing amenities of elderly persons in some parts of the country.

The Elderly Living Alone
People living alone are even less well equipped with water and sanitation facilities than other elderly households (see Table 2.4). 21% of the elderly living alone do not have any piped water as compared with 15% of all elderly households: 47% do not have a bath or shower (as compared with 38%) and 38% do not have an internal toilet as compared with 31%.

Power [18] found that 25% of the elderly living alone had problems with draughts and 20% had problems with dampness. He also found that only 3% of such persons had any central heating in their houses.

House Ownership
Ireland has one of the highest owner occupation rates in Europe, estimated at 76.8% in 1981. [19] This rate is still increasing while both the public and private rented sectors continue to decline as a proportion of the total housing stock. The relative importance of owner occupation in Ireland stems from a number of factors. Chief among these are historical and cultural factors which have been reinforced by the various schemes of state aid to the owner occupier.

In Ireland, in 1980, 43% of all households owned their dwellings outright and 33% owned their dwellings with a mortgage. However, 70% of all rural households owned their dwellings outright, compared with only 41% of urban households. [20]

House Ownership Amongst the Elderly
The owner occupied proportion among elderly person households is slightly higher than average, but the proportion who owned their dwellings outright is far higher than the average, 67% as compared with 43%. Table 2.6 gives a breakdown of the tenure of elderly person households.

The relatively high level of owner-occupation among elderly households presents certain problems. In some cases ownership can be a liability for the less active and less prosperous elderly person. He or she may lack the skill, initiative, financial resources or the physical capacity to undertake the necessary repairs and maintenance or to provide adequate heating in bigger and, frequently, run-down older houses. Possible ways by which elderly persons can overcome some of these problems are discussed in Chapters 8 and 9.

Homeless Elderly People
According to the best information available, there are about 3,000 homeless*

---

*The only definition of homeless currently extant in Irish law is that of *The 1824 Vagrancy Act* which uses the term "a person wandering abroad without visible means of support". It is considered useful here to indicate two other

30

Table 2.6: *Tenure of Elderly Persons Households by Age of Head, 1980*

	Age of Head		Single Person Households by Age of Head	
	65 and over	80 and over	65 and over	80 and over
Average number of rooms per household	4.7	4.6	4.2	4.1
Percentage tenure breakdown: %				
Owned outright	67.0	64.7	62.2	55.0
Owned—tenant purchase	8.2	3.6	5.7	4.4
Owned with mortgage	4.3	1.2	2.1	2.0
Rented, local authority	10.3	13.1	14.0	16.0
Rented, private				
furnished	1.9	3.8	4.0	6.0
unfurnished	5.9	9.6	8.1	13.3
Rent free	2.3	3.9	3.8	3.4
All tentures	100.0	100.0	100.0	100.0

Source: *Incomes of the Elderly in Ireland: And an Analysis of the States Contribution,* National Council for the Aged, 1984 Appendix 2 Table 15.

definitions. First, *The Housing (Homeless Persons) Bill,* submitted to Seanad Eireann in April 1983. It defines a person as homeless if:—
(1) (a) He or any person who might reasonably be expected to reside with him (i) has no accommodation and is vulnerable as a result of old age, mental illness, handicap or physical disability, pregnancy or other special reason and/or (ii) has no fixed abode and/or (iii) is usually resident in common lodging houses, refuges, night shelters or hostels and/or (iv) solely because of having no alternative accommodation, is forced to reside in a general or psychiatric hospital, a county home or other such institution; or
(b) he has accommodation but he cannot secure entry to it or it is probable that occupation of it will lead to violence from some other person residing in it; or
(c) his accommodation consists of a moveable structure, vehicle or vessel designed or adapted for human habitation and there is no place where he is entitled or permitted both to place it and to reside in it.

31

people in Ireland. A substantial proportion of these are elderly. Those runn-ing some night shelters, hostels or offering similar accommodation see them-selves as geared mainly towards providing for the needs of the elderly home-less.

The following were the percentages of residents who were homeless elderly* in a small selected number of night shelters/residential homes in September 1984 based on a single-night survey: [21]

Table 2.7: *Percentage of Residents in 5 Selected Night Shelters/Residential Houses Aged 50 Years and Over on a Selected Night*

	Dublin Simon Night Shelter	Residential Houses	Galway Night Shelter	Cork Night Shelter	Dundalk shelter/ house
% Aged 50 60	28.3	33.0	37.5	14.2	18.5
% Aged 60 70	7.5	60.0	6.0	25.0	11.1
% over 70	1.8	6.6	—	3.5	14.8

Source: *Single-Night Survey, Simon Community, 1984.*

(2) For the purpose of this Act, a person is threatened with homelessness if it is likely that within 28 days he will become homeless and in need of accommodation as defined in subsection (1) of this section.

A further definition is available from T*he Constitution of the District of Columbia, U.S.* as ratified on November 6, 1984:
"Sec 4: Definition of Homeless. A person shall be considered homeless of
   (a)   The person has no present possessory interest in an accommodation and lacks the means necessary to obtain such interest; or
   (b)   The person has a possessary interest in an accommodation but
      (1)   The person is unable to secure entry to that accommodation, or
      (2)   Occupation of the accommodation would likely lead to vio-lence from another occupant.

* It should be noted that in many instances homeless people tend to become old prematurely.

In Dundalk, one resident had recently applied for housing and been turned down. One in Galway was 'under investigation', the rest had not applied because, in the opinion of the Project Leader, they "did not consider themselves eligible". All of Cork Simon's 28 night shelter residents had made housing applications. Four of the applications were approved, including three for SHARE. (See Chapter 4) Of the Dublin night shelter's 53 residents, 23 had applied for housing, including eight over 50. They had been allocated between 22 and 30 points, 20 less than what was necessary for low-demand housing. According to the Project Leader there, the majority would be able or willing to take up sheltered or public housing.

These figures suggest that there is a significant number of elderly homeless people whose chances of obtaining public housing are, at best, dim.

This would appear to be in line with data from elsewhere. The *Report of the Joint Working Group on Homelessness* [22] (Northern Ireland Office, August 1984) found that 18% of Northern Ireland's homeless population was aged 56-65, and 21% were over 65. This was well above the proportions of those age cohorts in the general population, which were 12% and 16% respectively. 49% of the 56-65 age group had been homeless for over two years. The picture that emerges here again, is one of an elderly homeless population institutionalised in the night shelters, unable to move to public or supported housing.

British data reinforces this picture. The 1983 Department of the Environment Survey [23] showed that 27% of its study were aged 60-70 and 12% over 70. A 1982 Government Survey [24] found that 25% were aged 50-65 and 8% over 65. An earlier report on the homeless [25] found 22% aged 60-70 and 10% over 70.

The question of the provision of public housing for homeless elderly people is discussed in Chapter 3.

CHAPTER 3

PUBLIC HOUSING PROVISION FOR THE ELDERLY

Introduction

The Housing Acts [1] make it the duty of every housing authority to ascertain the extent of the need for dwellings at least every five years and to assess the adequacy of the supply and the prospective demand for housing. The *1968 Care of the Aged* report gave considerable attention to the housing of elderly people and recommended that housing authorities should include a special survey of the housing needs of elderly persons in every five yearly general assessment of housing needs, which they are obliged to carry out under the Housing Act, 1966. [2] In addition, the report recommended that a specific percentage of all new Local Authority dwellings should be allocated to aged persons. "Initially a minimum of 10% should be the aim". [3] The special features of old persons dwellings are smaller size and convenience of access to electrical sockets, switches and door handles. With relative minor adaptions they also incorporate provision for reasonable access by a wheelchair. They frequently have ground floor accommodation only, although this has certain disadvantages — noise, interference, burglaries. In some instances provision for the elderly is made in schemes with younger neighbours, thus broadening their range of contacts and company and giving greater protection.

Some old persons' dwellings are built as sheltered housing schemes and many have alarm/communication systems installed. For example, approximately 60% of Dublin Corporation's dwellings for senior citizens come into this category. [4] Chapter 5 contains a discussion on some aspects of *sheltered housing schemes* for elderly persons.

Local Authority Provision for the Elderly

Table 3.1 gives a breakdown of local authority provision for elderly persons for the period 1972-1982.

Table 3.1: *Local Authority Housing Provisions, 1972-1982*

Year	Annual number of housing units provided	Special units provided for elderly persons (including demountable)	Special units represented as % of total units
1972	5,902	390	10.01
1973	6,072	600	9.88
1974	6,746	670	9.93
1975	8,794	875	9.95
1976	7,263	763	10.50
1977	6,333	893	14.10
1978	6,073	925	15.23
1979	6,214	681	10.96
1980	5,984	625	10.40
1981	5,681	631 (120 demountable)	11.10
1982	5,686	550 (121 demountable)	9.67

Source: Department of the Environment, Special Tabulation for The National Council for the Aged, 1984.

The recommended figure of 10% housing allocation for aged persons has generally been met each year since 1972 and in some years well surpassed.

Table 3.2: *Number of Old People's Proposed Dwellings at 31.12.1982*

	Ordinary	Demountable	Total
Under construction	919	43	962
At tender	651	29	680
In planning	1,483	118	1,681

Source: Department of the Environment, Special Tabulation for The National Council for the Aged, 1984.

The number of approved applications from the elderly for dwellings at 31st December 1982 was 5,797 and involved 7,485 persons. This compares with 5,571 approved applications in 1981 involving 7,637 persons. [5]

The total number of old persons' dwellings in stock at 31st December 1982 was 10,196. The average time-scale that these dwellings will be occupied is ten years, and since they may not be sold, the stock of special old persons' dwellings will continue to rise as the number available for re-letting are added to those newly built. However, it should be noted that the life span of demountable dwellings is limited, they are generally remote, and the possibility of re-letting is not a real one in many instances. While the specific number of demountables in the current stock is not known, it can be roughly estimated, on the basis of the figures for 1981 and 1982, that 20% of the old persons' dwellings currently in stock are of the demountable, chalet variety.

It should also be noted that approved waiting lists cannot be regarded as a full measure of the extent of housing needs among the elderly, since some elderly persons in need have not been identified as such, for example, some people in privately owned or rented accommodation and homeless elderly persons.

The adequacy of the 10% allocation which has now become the norm for local authority provision for elderly persons, is, in the Council's view, likely to be inadequate in the coming years due to a number of factors as follows:

1. The 7.5% projected increase (Table 1.7) in the elderly population in the period up to 2006 will create greater demand for housing among the elderly.
2. The trend for greater numbers of elderly persons to live alone or in man and wife household is likely to continue up to 2006. (See Appendix 3).
3. The increased role for sheltered housing schemes in the care of the aged will create demand for provision by local authorities of such schemes.
4. The continuing problem of homeless elderly persons will need to be dealt with more effectively by local authorities.
5. The housing needs of the elderly vary very much from region to region and from county to county. Counties and regions with a high population of elderly persons (Table 1.3 and 1.4) require a higher rate of local authority allocations for the elderly. While detailed information on current local rates of provision is not available to the Council indications are that some regions and counties are less appropriately provided for in relation to local authority allocations for the elderly than others. It may also be the case that there is over provision in some areas.
6. There appears to be a growing number of people between the ages of forty and sixty who live in private rented accommodation and who do not have security of tenure (e.g. childless couples on a low income or single people) and who consequently are likely to require public authority housing.

Public Housing Policy and Homeless Elderly Persons

The issue of homelessness among elderly persons was referred to in Chapter 2. The Council recognises that this group, while representing a relatively small proportion of all elderly persons, are a particularly deprived group who require special provision for their accommodation by housing authorities and by other relevant agencies.

Most homeless people, of whatever age, do not choose to be homeless. Their homelessness is often either a product of their poverty or lack of secure accommodation or lack of income or work — or a combination of these factors. Personal and psychiatric factors often play their part. That homelessness is rooted in poverty and lack of choice of accommodation is borne out by research into homelessness. Although mental illness and alcoholism are often associated with the homeless, these problems tend to be consequent upon homelessness rather than a causative factor. A British Department of Environment Survey [6] found that only 11% of the homeless suffered from mental illness at their last settled base, and only a further 2% suffered from substance abuse at their last settled base. Mental illness among the homeless, where it has occurred, has generally been either a product of the stress of homelessness or, alternatively, is to be found among people who were improperly deinstitutionalised or who should perhaps be institutionalised. [7]

Once homeless it is very difficult to emerge from a situation of homelessness. The current operation of the supplementary welfare allowance does not facilitate a homeless person to move rapidly into the private rented sector. [8]

For example, it would appear that although £5 is set as the maximum rent allowance that can be paid without Ministerial approval, this has in fact become a norm, despite the fact that this is not in spirit with the guidelines issued to community welfare officers. Permission to pay more than £5 does not appear to be often sought, though it is normally granted when it is. In addition one health board (the Southern) appears to have a policy of paying either flat desposits or ESB connections, but not both. Most homeless people therefore become dependent on the network of night shelters, hostels and county homes.

The bulk (93%) of accommodation for homeless persons is provided by voluntary organisations. Despite the best efforts of these organisations to provide as high a quality of service for the homeless as they can, there are drawbacks to this type of provision. Many such organisations find it hard to maintain their services on extremely limited budgets. Places are often not allocated on a permanent basis; there is little privacy; residents must often be out during the day; and living conditions in some shelters are poor.

Most homeless people have very little opportunity of obtaining public

37

housing and consequently their problems are exacerbated as they become older. Some local housing authorities absolutely refuse to consider homeless for housing at all, insisting they are the responsibility of the health boards. They in turn may insist they are a housing problem. As a result of their non-eligibility for housing, the conditions of homeless people deteriorate further.

Even those homeless people for whom the local authorities do accept responsibility are normally made a low priority. In a submission to Dublin Corporation in January 1984, the Dublin Simon Community [9] detailed cases of elderly residents whose point allocations were so low that they stood little opportunity of housing for many years. This included a pensioner aged 69, who applied for housing in 1979 and was allocated 22 points in 1983. But the threshold for low-demand housing is 50 points and she has been told that, as it is, she is being much more favourably treated than a male shelter resident of similar age. As a result, homeless people are left in a most precarious position, particularly in times of severe seather and snow. At best, the elderly homeless will age prematurely; at worst, they will succumn to exposure.

Points are not allocated for homelessness nor for sleeping rough, though they are for not having hot water to hand. Although there is a 'social conditions' clause in point allocations, there are no established guidelines for its interpretation, unlike the 'medical conditions' clause. It is also relevant to note that some local authorities do, mistakenly consider hostels and shelters as adequate forms of housing. As a result of these factors, the housing needs of the elderly homeless have been severely underestimated.

Doubt has sometimes been cast on the will or ability of homeless people to manage their own independent housing. However, there is no evidence that homeless people require any greater medical or social work support in the course of their placement in their own independent housing than any other sector of the community. In rehousing hostel users in local authority housing in the years 1978-82, Glasgow City Council found that over 90% sustained their tenancies. [10] In a comprehensive survey of the city's hostel users, it was found that over 80% of respondents preferred a house or flat of their own, only 17% preferring to remain in hostels. [11]

Arising from its concern for the homless elderly, the Council supports the principle of a Homeless Persons Act that would require local authorities to accept housing responsibility for all homeless persons. Homelessness in this context is taken to mean that of an individual elderly person who:
(a) applies for or authorises an application on his/her behalf for local authority housing;
(b) cannot otherwise make provision for his/her housing needs from his/her own resources.

38

Two points of view were expressed concerning the need for further definition of the ability of an individual homeless person to maintain an independent tenacy. They were as follows:

(a) The individual should be required to show ability to maintain an independent tenancy.

(b) Such a requirement would be discriminatory and unnecessary.

The Council endorses the findings of the Ad Hoc Committee on the homeless established under the aegis of the Department of Health which reported in December 1984. [12] This report advocated an increased level of co-operation and liaison between health boards and housing authorities. It sets out guidelines by which statutory agencies responsible for the care and accommodation of homeless people may be enabled "to respond more quickly and more decisively to problem cases that come before them."

The Council notes and welcomes the circular letter sent by the Department of the Environment to each housing authority in February 1985 requesting housing authorities to take certain actions which are seen as more effectively catering for the housing needs of the homeless.[13] In particular, the Council welcomes the idea of housing authorities nominating an officer to liaise with health boards and voluntary bodies on individual cases of homelessness. In this respect the Council believes that there is a need for a greater variety of accommodation to meet the needs of some elderly persons, for example persons with psychiatric or alcohol or drug related problems who cannot cope on their own. Appropriate accommodation and ongoing grants should be made available to voluntary organisations to provide half-way houses and/or small hostel accommodation for people in these categories.

The Council also notes the recent publication of the Housing (Miscellaneous Provisions) Bill, 1985 which requires housing authorities to make suitable accommodation available for homeless persons.

Need for a More Wide-ranging System of Local Authority Allocation to the Elderly

The Council recommends that a more wide-ranging system of allocation that currently exists should be adopted by local authorities in relation to the letting of houses to the elderly. Such a system should incorporate consideration not only of factors of overcrowding and unfitness, but also of significant social, medical and environmental factors, such as:

1. age, with special reference to those aged 75 years and over;
2. circumstances relating to living alone and/or isolation;
3. suitability for housing, following appropriate assessment, of persons already in long-stay residential institutions;
4. homelessness, or being forced to reside in hostels, night shelters or lodging houses because of no other place to go;

39

5. the position of elderly people who are evicted or who are likely to be evicted from private rented accommodation because of their inability to pay rent;
6. the desirability of facilitating some isolated older people moving to villages or centres of population;
7. those whose medical condition is likely to be adversely affected by the unsuitablity of their present accommodation;
8. the desirability of housing elderly persons in their own area.

The Counicl suggests that, in considering these factors, housing authorities might have regard to special reports of the Director of Community Care for the area.

The Council also takes the view that criteria governing the important 'social conditions' factor in considering housing applications must be clarified. This process should be done in consultation with the appropriate personnel and voluntary organisations involved with the relevant types of applicants.

The Council notes that in Dublin housing points may be allocated on exceptional compassionate grounds (See Appendix 4).

The Council considers that there is likely to be a need for the provision of greater numbers of smaller dwellings (with 2 bedrooms) by local authorities for older persons (including married couple households) who would welcome such dwellings. This could free larger dwellings for letting to the larger families. The idea of local authorities accommodating elderly persons currently in the private sector in smaller local authority dwellings offers interesting possibilities for more efficient use of existing housing stock. In this way local authorities could acquire bigger properties from elderly owner-occupiers in return for rehousing them. These bigger properties could then be let to younger families. While many elderly persons living in larger houses do not wish to move, it is likely that if smaller houses and flats were more readily available more people would be prepared to move than is currently the case.

The appropriate size for housing units for the elderly should, in the Council's view, receive further consideration by local authorities with a view to providing two bedrooms where possible. In addition further consideration should be given to establishing the most appropriate size for local authority housing schemes for elderly persons.

40

CHAPTER 4

HOUSING BY VOLUNTARY ASSOCIATIONS

Introduction

A significant growth occurred in the voluntary housing sector in Ireland during the 1970's and voluntary associations and bodies have built a number of housing-for-the-elderly schemes on a limited scale around the country. These have usually been in the range of five to twenty five units and are available on a rental basis with most of their tenants paying relatively low rents. The work is carried out by social service groups, various denominational, religious and charitable groups, and other types of independent non-profit housing associations and trusts. At present there are 80 voluntary groups with approved status from the Department of the Environment to provide this type of housing. Such groups may qualify under Section 12 of the 1966 Housing Act (see Appendix 5) for loans from local authorities for the provision of rent accommodation either by way of new building or by rehabilitation of existing buildings. In addition to the financial assistance provided by the local authorities the regional health boards provide or contribute towards the provision of a range of community care service for sheltered housing tenants. This assistance, however, operates largely on an ad hoc basis. The success of voluntary housing associations and other voluntary groups in providing accommodation for the elderly, while not on a par with the level of provision in Great Briatain and Northern Ireland, nonetheless deserves consideration and offers interesting possibilities for the future provision of housing for the elderly in Ireland.

V .untary Housing Provision for the Elderly

At present there are about 1,850 rental dwelling units (approx. 1,200 for the elderly) provided by voluntary housing associations.

Ten of the groups currently with the Department of the Environment approved status are, under the aegis of Catholic Religious Orders, providing over 300 places for the elderly and elderly handicapped. The Iveagh Trust,

Dublin which has been in existence since the beginning of the century, has 813 units in total, with a significant number of units currently occupied by elderly persons.

The Society of St. Vincent de Paul provides schemes specifically for the elderly and elderly handicapped at Ballinamore, Castlebar, Charlestown, Drumshambo, Galway and has proposed a scheme for Sandymount, Dublin. The SHARE (Schoolboys Harness Aid for the Relief of the Elderly) group in Cork provides accommodation for 124 elderly and 15 elderly handicapped. Some of these agencies provide accommodation for other categories of persons including handicapped and young married couples in the same complex as the elderly. In the 'SHARE Model' Cork Corporation supplies the services sites and since the houses or flats are built on Corporation property they are owned and maintained by the Corporation.

The Role of Trade Unions

It is worth noting what appears to be the complete absence of any significant Trade Union involvement in the non-profit voluntary housing movement in Ireland. This also appears to be the case in Britain, but is in noticeable contrast to the role of the trade unions as the original sponsors and organisers of the non-profit/social/co-operative housing associations elsewhere in Europe. They are still involved at national levels in social housing federation in several EEC countries.

The Council wishes to draw attention to the fact that, unlike the trade union movement in other countries, the Irish trade unions have not involved themselves in housing services for their members. There appears to be a particularly worthwhile potential for this type of trade union activity in the case of housing for the elderly, thereby keeping up the social links with retired members.

It is certainly regrettable that the organisational experience of trade unions is not brought to bear more directly on this issue, although it must be recognised that individual trade union members do participate in other voluntary/social service associations and, indeed, some members are elected representatives of local authorities. This experience could be put to practical use in a direct way through the promotion of non-profit voluntary housing schemes.

Funding

Voluntary groups which had obtained approved status from the Department of the Environment could, up to February 1984, apply to the local authority for a loan not exceeding 90% of the net cost of the provision of self-contained housing units by way of new buildings, or improvement or conversion of existing buildings. A rental subsidy was also available to assist towards the outgoings, including loan repayments of each dwelling. The subsidy was limited to 50% of the economic rent of a new local authority house built in the same area in the preceding year.

A new scheme of financial assistance for the provision of housing by voluntary bodies was announced by the Minister for the Environment in February 1984. This can be summarised as follows:

1. Assistance to voluntary bodies providing housing for the elderly and other disadvantaged categories is now in the form of loans by housing authorities to meet 80% of the cost of an eligible project (including site), subject to a maximum loan equivalent to £16,000 per unit of accommodation. No capital grant is payable.

2. On condition that the accommodation is used in accordance with paragraph 3, loan charges on a loan under 1 above will be recouped in full to a housing authority by the Department, so relieving the voluntary body of the full liability for loan charges. All other costs of maintaining and managing the project rest with the voluntary body.

3. To qualify for a loan 75% at least, of the units of accommodation must be rented to:
   (a)   elderly* persons eligible for local authority housing or institutional care at public expense; or
   (b)   handicapped persons, homeless persons, deserted or battered wives, single parent families and families on approved waiting lists for local authority houses who could not reasonably be expected to secure adequate housing accommodation from their own resources. (The homeless are included as a new category).

4. A voluntary body is required to enter into a legal agreement with the local authority regarding the loan, and specifically regarding repayment in the event of the accommodation not continuing to be let to eligible persons under the scheme, and regarding disposal of the property while a balance remains outstanding on the loan.

The average new dwelling unit provided by voluntary groups currently costs in the region of £20,000 including the cost of the site and the cost of providing welfare and warden accommodation. Thus, most units will qualify for the maximum local authority loan of £16,000. This loan is effectively the equivalent of an 80% capital subsidy to voluntary housing associat-

*In general, persons of 60 years or over may, in the renting of accommodation be regarded as 'elderly'. However, it is not intended that this age limit be applied in an absolutely rigid manner and persons below that age might be accommodated where the housing authority considers such a course is justified.

ions and, as such, should open the way for greater activity by voluntary housing associations in the future. The fact that local authorities can, under the new scheme, recoup, in full, the loan charges from the Department of the Environment should facilitate greater involvement by local authorities in voluntary housing schemes. Indeed the success of voluntary housing in Britain and Northern Ireland can be largely attributed to (i) the high level of capital grants (90% of capital costs) available to voluntary associations from the relevant housing authorites and (ii) state financial aid to such associations for ongoing current costs which is virtually 100%.

In Northern Ireland state aid, in various forms, for housing associations started at about £0.5m STG in 1976 and in the current year reached £43m STG. The N.I. housing associations currently manage some 2,000 units of sheltered accommodation for the elderly.

In the Irish context, the new scheme means that voluntary associations will have to raise something in the region of £4,000 per unit of the capital cost, where the capital unit cost is £20,000. For a ten house scheme this could be as much as £40,000, which is a very significant sum for many voluntary bodies. The introduction of V.A.T., at 5% on building a further adds to the capital cost to the voluntary organisation. In addition there are the ongoing costs of maintenance and the provision of welfare services.

While the current system of grant aid to voluntary associations is seen as a major step forward, the Council takes the view that the development and expansion of voluntary housing in Ireland will continue to be inhibited by inadequate funding to cover not only the capital costs (as referred to above) but also such current costs as maintenance, insurance, welfare personnel, heat and light.

The Council recommends that defined subsidy schemes should be established to cater for running costs of voluntary housing for the elderly. Such subsidy schemes would cover:

(a) Current running costs (e.g. heat, light, maintenance, insurance, caretaking) under Section 12 ('Periodic Contribution') of the 1966 Housing Act.

(b) Costs of welfare caring services (meals, home helps) under Section 65 of the Health Act 1953.

The lack of such a scheme frequently results in voluntary organisations being beset with continuous financial crises and a consequent inability to engage in forward planning. This being the case, such organisations then find themselves unable to fulfil their caring function adequately, thus defeating their primary purpose in being involved in such schemes at all.

Responsibilities of Voluntary Housing Associations

The precise responsibilities of voluntary housing associations in relation to the elderly is not altogether clear. Given that some elderly persons who move to sheltered accommodation are eventually likely to become unsuited to such accommodation, the Council takes the view that the management committee of the voluntary housing association should have to take some responsibility for seeking places in other forms of accommodation for their tenants or residents. This is particularly important when such residents, who have no next-of-kin or person designated to manage their affairs, become too frail, physically or mentally, to cope within their complexes. At present, some committees get their medical officer, or the tenant's own doctor, to transfer the tenant to an acute hospital, then refuse to have him/her back. In some instances committees may even 'wash their hands' of any further obligations or responsibility, inferring their former residents are the responsibility of the hospital from the time of admission onwards. Given that these associations should be endeavouring to provide a 'substitute home' for the elderly, some form of 'family' obligation devolves on to the committees of management. For this reason they should have a direct link with the director of community care in their areas and also with the hospital-based geriatric service. Such links must involve "two way traffic", including adequate financial and other supports for voluntary associations, if the concept of community care is to work properly.

Conclusion

The Council sees a potentially important role for voluntary housing associations in the provision of housing for the elderly, particularly in view of the increased importance being given to sheltered housing in the care of the elderly in the community. The local community involvement in the building and running of housing schemes for the elderly provides for a flexible and sensitive approach to these housing needs. It also raises the general community awareness of the needs of the elderly and thus enhances the quality of their lives in the community. The Council, however, wishes to emphasise that this role will only be realised if statutory financial assistance to housing associations is such as to include realistic subsidies for both the current and capital costs of their housing schemes. The Council also believes that the development of voluntary housing in Ireland will continue to be contingent on local authorities assuming a developmental role by involving voluntary associations in every possible manner, viz. the provision of sites; the payment of loans in instalments to eliminate the high costs of bridging finance; the rationalisation of legal procedures; flexibility in relation to technical requirements, especially in the conversion of existing dwellings, while retaining appropriate standards. This approach would also serve to eliminate the present competition for scarce resources between the local authorities' own housing schemes and schemes operated by voluntary associations.

CHAPTER 5

SHELTERED HOUSING

Introduction

The idea of sheltered housing is an old one and can be traced back to the Alms Houses of the Middle Ages and the Cottage Homes of the nineteenth century in Britain. Since the Second World War housing policy in many European countries has seen a series of Acts, Circulars and Bulletins encouraging the expansion of specially designed and located dwellings for the elderly. Alongside the concept of the smaller flat and bungalow for elderly persons has grown the idea of sheltered housing development in a number of these countries. Such housing is variably referred to as specialist, congregate, warden-controlled and sheltered, the latter term being the one used throughout this report.

Sheltered Housing may consist of a number of flats in a single building or cluster of bungalows. Each flat or bungalow is small and specially designed for access and mobility by frail elderly persons and is completely self-contained with all the facilities necessary for the elderly person or couple to cater fully for themselves. General supervision by a warden living in the building, with a built-in call system and in regular communication with all the residents, is a normal feature of the sheltered housing unit. Communal facilities, including communal meals, are sometimes provided. The location of the unit, close to shops, transport, church and other services, such as family doctor, public health nurse, day centres and home help service is important. Sweden, Denmark and the Netherlands have made a definite policy decision to phase out residential homes for the elderly in favour of more sheltered housing projects and community services. [1] As far back as 1962, Peter Townsend, in his monumental study of institutional care in Britain, *The Last Refuge,* recommended the building of sheltered housing as the major priority in order to "improve housing standards and eliminate past deficiencies". [2] He suggested that a target of 50 grouped sheltered housing places per 1,000 elderly should be set. In 1972 the Scottish Home and Health Department set a target of 25 places per 1,000 elderly population[3]

46

Belton states that sheltered housing has become "central to the care of the elderly in the community". [4] In England and Wales approximately 5% of people over retirement age now live in some form of sheltered housing. [5]

Sheltered Housing Provision for the Elderly

The 1968 Care of the Aged report, as we have seen in Chapter 3, advocated that local authorities allocate a percentage of dwellings specifically for elderly persons. In addition, the report recommended that housing authorities should make provisions for sheltered housing "where it is not feasible to meet the housing needs of the elderly in their own or similar houses". [6] The figure for the total number of sheltered housing units provided to date by local authorities in Ireland is not available. Limerick Corporation completed a scheme of sheltered housing for the aged as early as 1973 and reported close liaison with the health authorities and voluntary organisations in the planning of the scheme. [7] Dublin Corporation, the largest housing authority in the country, currently houses some 2,000 (i.e. 60% of its elderly tenants in sheltered housing schemes. [8] These schemes have a minimum of 40 units, are warden controlled and have a built-in alarm/communications system. The duties of the wardens include assisting the elderly tenants, summoning help, reporting complaints, and checking daily to ensure the safety of all residents.

Sheltered housing schemes for the elderly have also been provided by voluntary housing associations and groups throughout the country which have been active in this area, particularly in the last ten years. (See Chapter 4).

Until very recently private developers have shown little interest in the field of sheltered housing for the elderly but schemes such as the Retirement Village at Clonmannon House, Ashford, Co. Wicklow can be expected to become more prevalent in the coming years. The Council is of the view that the private sector should be encouraged to provide more sheltered housing schemes for elderly persons who can afford it, thereby increasing the range of housing options available to elderly persons who are currently owner-occupiers.

Role of Sheltered Housing

Improved housing quality, greater ease of mobility and the security of a warden are three of the main advantages usually attributed to sheltered accommodation. A report of a survey of sheltered tenants in Housing Executive schemes in Belfast gives the reasons for tenants moving to sheltered accommodation. These are summarised in Table 5.1

47

Table 5.1: *Reasons for moving to sheltered accommodation, 1982*

Dwelling too small	Dwelling too big	Mobility problems	Cooking/ laundry diffs.	Unsuitable heating	Dwelling in poor condition	Security of a warden	Lone- liness	Nearer friends/ relatives	Redevelop- ment	Better social environ- ment	Other
4.2	21.4	30.5	7.4	5.3	28.8	44.6	20.4	12.3	27.4	8.1	14.0

Source: *Sheltered Tenant Survey*, a Study of NI Housing Executive Schemes in Belfast, DHSS, 1982, Table 3.6.

The feeling of security derived from the availability of a warden is stressed by a significant proportion of tenants (45%), while problems of mobility in the previous dwelling were mentioned by over 30% of tenants. Almost 29% stated that the previous dwelling was in poor condition, while 21% claimed that they moved because they found their accommodation too big for their needs.

Butler et al, commenting on the sheltered housing situation in Britain, refer to "the uneasy position that sheltered housing occupies between community living and residential living". [9] This 'uneasy position' also applies in the Irish context and stems from a lack of a clearly defined role for sheltered housing and of different interpretations of its role by different individuals and agencies. For example, the expectation of the community care and hospital services personnel regarding the role of sheltered housing may be quite different from that of local authority and voluntary services personnel. Some may see sheltered housing as catering for the medical needs of elderly people while others see no such role for sheltered housing. The position has been well summarised by Clayton:

> "some see it primarily as a welfare service to be provided only for the very frail; others believe it to be basically a housing service, but with a few social and welfare facilities added to help tenants maintain self-care, or think of it as a preventive service suitable for all elderly people. Some consider it to be on a ladder of increasingly comprehensive service along which people may move between residence in their old home and care in a hostel or hospital. Others see it as the place where an elderly person can stay from their 60's until, except in unusual circumstances, they die." [10]

A number of questions are frequently raised concerning the provision of sheltered housing. They include:

(i)   Should the elderly be treated as a separate/specialist group, thus perhaps pre-supposing and re-inforcing a particular view of them as frail, dependent? How far are the elderly a different group?

(ii)   Does sheltered housing in practice prevent the institutionalisation of elderly persons?

(iii) What are the effects of housing the elderly together? Does it create a ghetto and is this what old people want?

(iv)   What are the consequences for elderly people of warden and contact systems and do they become more dependent as a result? Do alarm systems lead to less social contact?

(v)   Would an emphasis on sheltered housing create a situation where the isolated rural elderly and the elderly being cared for by families would tend to be forgotten?

(vi)   How far should old people be encouraged/pressurised to move into

sheltered housing?
(vii)   Do people in sheltered housing get more or less domiciliary and other services than people living in other forms of housing?
(viii)   Are there people requiring continuing nursing care living in sheltered housing who should really be in hospital or long-term nursing homes?
(ix)   What is the most appropriate size for a sheltered housing scheme?

Many housing authorities in Britain are currently considering the need to provide "very sheltered" schemes (24 hours staff surveillance by up to as many as four wardens with facilities for up to 3 meals a day for tenants).[11] Boldy raises an important question in this respect:

"Does the advocacy of very sheltered schemes stem from the view that sheltered housing in its traditional form is incapable of caring for frail elderly tenants even with adequate support from health and social services or is it a recognition that such 'adequate support' will not be forthcoming?" [12]

In addition to the above general factors relating to the provision of sheltered housing, there are a number of specific issues relating to such provision in Ireland, which can be summarised as follows:

(i)   The extent to which sheltered housing fulfils more of a welfare need than a housing need has never been clearly defined in the Irish context.
(ii)   The range of dependency — social, physical, psychological — to be catered for in sheltered housing and the type and level of support services required to meet needs has not been clearly established.
(iii)   Despite a circular from the Department of the Environment in 1970, [13] suggesting that prototype plans for sheltered housing be prepared and some pilot schemes specifically designed for Irish conditions carried out, the development of such schemes has not been systematic.
(iv)   Very little information is currently available on the type of sheltered housing provision in Ireland. Little is known about the medical/social status of existing tenants or their needs or about the efficiency of the existing sheltered housing provision in meeting these needs.
(v)   The role, if any, to be played by the health boards in the planning and letting of sheltered housing has not been defined and appears to operate purely on an ad hoc basis.
(vi)   The role of the warden, which is inevitably related to the level of dependency among the tenants, has not been adequately defined and there appears to be inadequate training, relief help and supervision for wardens.
(vii)   The basic problem associated with the provision of sheltered housing in Ireland is the division of responsibility between two different authorities. The health authority identifies and has close contact with many of the people who need sheltered housing while the housing

authority has the responsibility to provide, maintain and supervise such housing. The medical, social, welfare and housing needs of the elderly person very often overlap.

Despite the various questions that have been raised above in relation to the provision of sheltered housing for the elderly, the Council is of the view that much greater emphasis should be placed on the provision of such housing as a centrally important link in the provision of community services for the elderly and the consequent reduction of the numbers going into institutional care. This is all the more important because of the projected increases in the numbers of elderly persons in the population aged 75 years and over. Sheltered housing units should be clearly located within a range of facilities and services which will help maintain the elderly person as a functionally active member of the community for as long as possible. This requires a high level of co-ordination between health boards, housing authorities and voluntary agencies,and between the hospital and community care programmes within the health boards.

There would also appear to be a need to provide more adequate training and supervision for wardens and to define more clearly their hours of work and responsibilities. At present, for example, in most instances there is no provision for cover periods when the warden is on "time off" or on annual leave or sick leave. It is likely that the provision of more effective training, scheduling and supervision for wardens would require the appointment of one or more full-time supervisors/co-ordinators, particularly by Dublin Corporation where there is a growing number of warden-controlled schemes.

The Council is not in a position to determine the national requirements for sheltered housing either in number or type because of:

(a) the lack of an accepted agreed understanding by the various agencies involved as to what constitutes sheltered housing;

(b) the related difficulty of identifying potential clients for sheltered housing;

(c) the lack of detailed information about the costs of providing adequate and appropriately designed, staffed and serviced sheltered housing accommodation.

The Council, therefore, recommends that an Inter-Departmental Working Group should be set up in order to examine and assess the role and contribution of sheltered housing — both statutory and voluntary — in the provision of accommodation and selected services for the elderly within an Irish context and to make recommendations accordingly. This Working Group should be comprised of representatives from both the Department of Health and the Department of the Environment and should consult with local authorities, health boards and voluntary housing associations currently providind sheltered accommodation for the elderly.

CHAPTER 6

PRIVATE RENTED ACCOMMODATION

Introduction

The private rented sector was traditionally an important source of housing for the poor and minority groups in the population. There has however, been a decline in the amount of all private rented accommodation available, together with a sizeable switch to furnished accommodation during the past 10 years, as can be seen from Table 6.1

Table 6.1: *Number of Privately Rented Dwelling Units 1971,-1981*
(In parentheses is percentage of total private dwellings)

	1971 %	1981 %
Rented unfurnished, other than from Local Authority	65,048 (9%)	33,429 (4%)
Rented furnished or part unfurmished	31,836 (4%)	55,942 (6%)
Total	96,884 (13%)	89,371 (10%)

Source: *Census of Population 1981,* Provisional Results, Bulletin 40, Central Statistics Office, Dublin.

In the ten year period from 1971 to 1981 there was an 8% decrease in the total number of privately rented dwellings in the country. During the same period there was a 76% increase in the number of furnished or part furnished dwellings.

In 1980 8% of all elderly person households were privately rented. This is somewhat lower than the percentage of dwellings privately rented in the total general population (10%). However, the percentage of privately rented elderly person dwellings where the head was living alone or aged 80 years and over was significantly higher, i.e. 12.1% and 13.4% respectively. In the case of elderly persons who are both living alone and aged 80 years and over the percentage in privately rented accommodation was as high as 19.3%. (See Table 6.2)

Table 6.2: *% of Elderly Person Households Privately Rented by Age of Head, 1980*

	All Elderly Person Households Age of Head		Single Person Households Age of Head	
	65 and over	80 and over	65 and over	80 and over
Furnished	1.9	3.8	4.0	6.0
Unfurnished	5.9	9.6	8.1	13.3
Total Private Rented	7.8	13.4	12.1	19.3

Source: *Incomes of the Elderly in Ireland: And An Analysis of the States Contribution.* National Council for the Aged, 1984.

In view of the fact that a considerable proportion of the private and rented accommodation referred to above is likely to be of the bed-sitter variety and consequently very unsuitable for elderly persons, the Council considers that local authorities should give special attention to elderly persons in such accommodation in the allocation of public housing to the elderly. (See Chapter 3)

Dwellings Formerly Subject to Rent Control
A significant proportion of elderly people living in private rented accommodation live in dwellings which were subject to rent control under the Rent Restrictions Acts in 1960 and 1982. The Housing (Private Rented Dwellings Act), 1982 introduced a modified form of control.

This Act provides for a measure of security of tenure for tenants of private rented dwellings and their families. It also provides for a method of determining rent when the landlord and tenant disagree. In addition, it provides for compensation for tenants on quitting a dwelling and a rent allowance scheme for tenants, administered by the Department of Social Welfare. Under the Act, the District Court also deals with applications for recovery of possession of a dwelling by a landlord and with compensation for tenants on quitting a dwelling.

Rent Tribunal

The Housing (Private Rented Dwellings) (Amendment) Act, 1983 led to the establishment of the Rent Tribunal in 1983. The Rent Tribunal substitutes for the District Court in determining the terms of the tenancy. The District Court continues to deal with matters assigned to it under the 1982 Act. The terms of tenancy include not only the rent for the dwelling, but also agreements concerning the use of the dwelling, such as the responsibility for repairs, insurance and any other charges that might need to be paid in respect of the dwelling. Where the landlord and tenant cannot reach agreement on the rent for a dwelling, either may apply to the Rent Tribunal to have the rent fixed. Applications are determined by the Tribunal on the basis of written submissions made to it and oral hearings held by it.

The dwelling which is the subject of the application is inspected by members of the Tribunal. The Tribunal will hold an oral hearing if either party requests it, but the case may be determined solely on the basis of written submissions. The new rent as decided by the Tribunal will come into force on the first gale day (the first normal day for paying rent) after the landlord has registered the new rent with the housing authority in which the dwelling is situated as required by regulations made under the 1982 Act.

The Department of Social Welfare administers a scheme of rent allowances for tenants of formerly controlled dwellings suffering hardship as a result of an increase in rent. To be eligible for a rent allowance the rent must have been fixed by the Rent Tribunal (or by the District Court under the 1982 Act) and the means of the tenant must be below specified levels. In all cases the tenant will be required to pay the existing rent or £3.80 whichever is the greater. The maximum allowance is payable to a single or widowed person whose means are not more than £51 weekly. The maximum allowance is payable to a married couple whose means are not more than £90 weekly.

The Council welcomes the setting up of the Tribunal which is much less formal than the courts system and consequently more satisfactory for elderly persons. It is premature to evaluate the effectiveness of the Tribunal in dealing with all the problems of the elderly relating to rented accommodation. The Council, however, makes a number of observations, as follows:

(i) The Tribunal only sets the terms of tenancy and rent. These terms of tenancy and rent may still have to go to the District Court to be enforced.

(ii) The current income limit for the rent allowance creates a problem of insecurity for some elderly people who are forced to use their life-long savings to pay the new rent.

(iii) It is still not permissible for tenants to divide and/or sub-let rented accommodation. The Council believes that many people would live much more securely and purposefully if they could sub-let accommodation

54

that has become too big for their current requirements.

(iv) Due to the low rents paid to landlords in rent-controlled dwellings over the years, difficulties arose concerning maintenance and repairs. Some landlords are themselves elderly and also could not afford the high cost of repairs. Dampness, lack of heat and lack of basic sanitary facilities result causing severe hardship to many tenants.

The Council notes that the Minister for the Environment had made new Regulations entitled 'Housing (Private Rented Dwellings) (Standards) Regulations 1984[1] which set standards in the formerly controlled rented dwellings sector. The Regulations require a landlord to ensure that the dwelling is maintained in a proper state of structural repair. They include details of the standard of repair required, services and other facilities to be provided, including bath or shower, w.c., piped water, drainage, avoidance of dampness and freezing of pipes, good repair and safety of gas and electricity instalments, removal of fumes, natural lighting and ventilation of rooms.

The landlord shall keep in good repair and safe working order all means of cooking, lighting and heating which are used by the "tenant in common with other persons". Repair and cleaning of stairs, cellars, yards, outbuildings, w.c., and basins, lighting of passage ways etc., used "by a tenant in common with other persons" are to be the responsibility of the landlord. But any breakage of glass in windows in any part of the dwelling of which a tenant has exclusive use does not have to be repaired by the landlord.

The new regulations came into operation on April 1st 1985. Where a tenancy agreement has been fixed by the District Court or by the Rent Tribunal or by agreement before the 1st April, 1985 and set out in written form in accordance with section 11 of the Act of 1982, landlords are not required to meet the new standards until 1st January, 1988, or when they next apply to the rent tribunal for a review of rent, whichever is sooner.

The Council welcomes the introduction of the new regulations but wishes to draw attention to some limitations.

1. The three-year intervening period before the regulations come into operation for many tenancies is likely to create continuing serious problems for elderly people whose dwellings are currently inadequately maintained;

2. It is likely that even under the new regulations many landlords will plead inability to bear the costs of severe deterioration to buildings.

Other Private Rented Dwellings

The Council does not have detailed information on the numbers of elderly persons living in other rented accommodation (i.e. not formerly controlled).

There are indications, however, that a sizeable number of elderly people live in such accommodation, much of which is inadequately maintained. tained.

A most detailed description of this sector was provided by Threshold in 1982. [2] Their insights and recommendations were based on their extensive casework in the private rented sector, both the formerly controlled sector and the uncontrolled sector. 6.2% of their casework with the controlled sector was with people over 60, including pensioners. This figure may underestimate the numbers of old people in this sector, for, being less mobile, they will be less inclined to travel to use the service.

The main findings [3] of this data were that 20% in the total study group considered their living conditions 'very bad' and 6% 'poor'. There were 972 cases of evictions in a 15 month period, accounting for 32.4% of the caseload. Problems of rent increase accounted for 18.8% and repairs for 10.7%. Over half those living in the uncontrolled sector had to share a bathroom/ w.c., 3% had none at all. For those whose principal problem was repairs, 28.5% needed multiple repairs, 21.8% structural repairs, and others had problems of water supply, heating, dampness and electricity. The poorest of those living in the private rented sector were spending 25% of their income on rent. The report stated:

"Without doubt, however, the most significant indicator of insecurity for tenants of furnished private rented accommodation is the ease with which they can be evicted. The landlord's right to evict the tenant has full backing in law and, regardless of the rights and wrongs of a case, the landlord will invariably secure an Order for Possession against the tenant".

"Apart from the constant fear of being evicted, and for reasons frequently outside the tenant's control, the most serious threat to the tenant's security of tenure is related to the ability to meet the rent demanded, since the choice is invariably between paying and leaving". [4]

It concluded that "the poor are heavily over-represented in the rented sector." [5]

Threshold considered the options for reforming the private rented sector. It took the view that the private rented sector did have a viable longterm and desirable role in the housing market, because it could efficiently meet the housing needs of particular groups. It argued that it was important to:

"safeguard the interests of existing private tenants, many of whom are elderly ... (and) provide a legislative framework which preserves a fair balance between the interests of tenants and landlords." [6]

Threshold recommended the establishment of Private Rented Housing Boards that would regulate tents, adjudicate on rent adjustment and act as an arbitration service. It also proposed compulsory written leases, controlled deposits, the right of court appeal against eviction, standardised eviction notices and statutory minimum standard bye-laws. The Council considers that an alternative and equally acceptable approach would be to extend the existing Rent Tribunal to this sector, but with these extended terms of reference. The Council recommends that the Department of the Environment draw up appropriate legislation with all due speed in order to instigate appropriate procedures to cater for problems associated with the non-controlled private sector.

CHAPTER 7

ALARM/COMMUNICATION SYSTEMS FOR THE ELDERLY

Introduction
The view that society takes towards the elderly at risk, coupled with the growing number of elderly persons living alone, whether by choice or because of other reasons, creates problems not only for the elderly themselves but also for concerned relatives and neighbours and for housing and health authorities. The elderly are sometimes frightened of falling and not being able to summon assistance. "Half the old people living alone are less than certain of their ability to summon help if taken ill suddenly." [1] Others fall and may not admit it in case they may be pressurised by relatives or health authorities to move out of their chosen abode. The fear of being attacked in their own homes and not being able to call for help is a constant pre-occupation for many elderly persons living alone in both urban and rural settings. Fire also continues to be a major hazard for many elderly persons living alone.

The Council recognises that there is no simple single solution to such problems facing the elderly who live alone. The issue is at once one of independence and one of protection for the elderly. Telephone contact and alarms systems provide a high level of emotional security for elderly persons but should be seen only as part of a comprehensive community effort to assist old people living alone. There is no substitute for good neighbourhood surveillance both on an informal and a formal basis. Constant and regular (daily) checking by neighbours, relatives and social services personnel is the single most important element in the reduction of risk among the elderly and disabled.

Telephone Contact
The Council recommends that many more elderly persons living alone in both urban and rural areas should be enabled to acquire a telephone or have easy access to one.

58

The majority of respondents (86%) in the 'Old and Alone' Survey had no telephones. Of those who had no telephones, 40% had no easy access to a working telephone. [2] The possession of a telephone appears to represent the best guarantee of being able to summon help in an emergency as is illustrated in Table 7.1

Table 7.1: *Possession of Telephone and Confidence in Ability to Summon Help*

	Sure of getting help %
Those having telephones	91
Those having access to telephones	50
Those having no telephone/no access	29

Source: Power B., *Old and Alone in Ireland*, 1982, Table 8.1.

Of those who have their own telephones 91% feel sure of being able to summon help in an emergency as compared with 50% of those who only have access to a telephone on someone else's premises or in a street or hall kiosk. The problem of not being able to summon help is more serious for those who have no access to a telephone.

' ... a mere 29% are confident of being able to get help in a hurry and the majority (60%) are certain that there is no way they could call anyone in the event of sudden illness.' [3]

Only 25% of those living in the countryside in the Republic of Ireland were sure of getting help if needed as compared to 65% of those living in city/town centres. (See Table 7.2).

Table 7.2: *Location of Dwelling and Confidence in Ability to Summon Help*

	Sure of getting help		
	N. Ireland	Republic	Total
City/town centre	77%	65%	69%
Elsewhere in city/town	65%	63%	63%
Village	56%	36%	40%
Countryside	46%	25%	28%

Source: Power B., *Old and Alone in Ireland*, 1982, Table 8.2.

59

Power states that "Old people living in the open countryside are least likely to have their own telephones although they are the group we may assume would have greatest need of this form of emergency communication". [4]

The Council welcomes the initiative that has been taken by Telecom Eireann in developing a system which would enable elderly or disabled people to summon help immediately in the event of a break-in or emergency without the need to lift a telephone. Such a system is operated by a portable watch-size button worn around the neck or alternatively by sensors placed by doors or windows which would trigger the alarm automatically. However such a system will be applicable in rural areas only if the present telephone network is widely extended and if appropriate round-the-clock contact centres are developed.

Other Alarm/Communication Systems

The earliest and simplest forms of alarm systems for the elderly were mechanical devices which registered as a flashing light or illuminated sign outside the person's house. These were simple to install and enabled the elderly person in distress to signal this fact to the outside world. These systems have become less popular since they also advertise the vulnerability of the occupier to any passer-by.

Electronic alarms of various kinds have become standard in many sheltered housing schemes. They link the tenant to a resident warden who is notified by an alarm buzzer or light when a tenant makes a call. Some of these systems have incorporated a two-way speech device.

In recent years there has been a significant development of dispersed or central-call alarm systems. These enable an elderly person to register an alarm call with somebody who is some distance away from him/her. Typically, the operator at central control registers the emergency and then relays the information to someone able to gain access and visit the elderly person in distress. Some sheltered housing schemes have a system by which they can switch the call from a sheltered housing tenant into the dispersed alarm network when the resident warden is off duty.

The newer alarm/communication systems provide new dimensions to security including fire warnings, temperature alerts if it drops very low and inactivity monitors. They may also provide a faster link to the Gardai, G.P.s and hospitals. In the modern systems when a call is received in the Aid Centre, a profile of the call appears automatically on the screen of the monitor giving details of the caller, that is, name and address, names of relatives, next of kin, G.P., public health nurse, health and other relevant details.

Some Existing Alarm Systems

(i) Dublin Corporation [5]

Since about 1967 a type of alarm system has been installed in all Warden Schemes by Dublin Corporation.

The quality and efficiency of the systems used in these schemes reflects the progress in technology over the years. The earlier schemes — about 25 in all — have the light/bell calling mechanisms while the more recent schemes — about 10 in all — have a sophisticated talk-back system with many possible extras to provide greater security for old people.

In 1984 some flats occupied by elderly persons were identified as being particularly vulnerable and a new alarm/communication system was installed. This system joins up a maximum of 32 flats in any one scheme via one telephone line to an Aid Centre which provides a 24 hours, seven-day-week answering service to the caller. The Aid Centre, supplied and manned by a commercial firm, has a profile of each of the old people who are linked to the centre. When a call for help comes in, the Centre can immediately identify the caller and the service the old person may require. The Corporation has already given approval to extend the system to 24 further flats.

The Council notes the relatively high cost of providing this system (approximately £300 per unit) and sees this as one of the major drawbacks of the system.

(ii) Wexford [6]

In Wexford an elaborate alarm system which is simple to use has been installed on a pilot basis in the homes of 13 elderly persons living alone. This system provides a direct 24 hour radio link to a central unit in the general hospital in the town. Here there are keys to the houses of all the elderly persons in the scheme. In addition to the key kept at the hospital, keys to each elderly person's house are also held by three persons (neighbours, friends or relatives) who have been nominated by the elderly person and who have their confidence. These persons can be contacted by the central unit in the hospital on the receipt of an alarm call and are in a position to check out the problem with the elderly person.

The unit in the elderly person's house can be activated by a portable push-button device worn around the neck or carried in the pocket around the house. There is a facility in the unit in the elderly person's house to call an ambulance directly if this is deemed to be necessary by whoever calls to the house. Some of the people involved in the scheme also have a 'passive alarm' which they activate every morning and night as an indication to the central unit that they do not require help. The Council considers that each local authority or health board, or preferably both conjointly, should explore the possibility of developing in the long-term an integrated alarm/communication system which would embrace and link-up all elderly persons at risk in both public and private housing. The needs of a particular area, for example, all of Dublin City and County could easily be serviced by one modern console in an Aid Centre which would provide a "Round the Clock" answering service. Many Aid Centres in Britain, administered by local authorities are covering large areas of population, for example, Hull, Leeds and Manchester. Such an integrated approach would seem to be in the interests of good management, economy and the provision of a more effective service to the elderly at risk.

Role of Alarm/Communication Systems

While welcoming the provision of alarm/communication systems, wherever practicable, the Council also wishes to introduce a note of caution. There is not enough solid evidence at present to support the statement that the provision of alarms will greatly reduce risks among the elderly. They may not be the universal panacea that some manufacturers of such alarm systems would lead us to believe. A study of some 200 elderly and disabled people reported in 1975 that 77% of the people did not use their alarm system in the emergencies they experienced. [7] Another study of 600 sheltered housing tenants carried out in 1980 demonstrated that almost as many people failed for some reason to make use of the alarm system in an emergency as actually did make use of it. [8]

Currently we do not know enough about the effects of alarm installations on elderly people. While the emphasis has been placed on the positive aspects of such systems it is necessary to consider the following questions:

Does the ownership of an alarm adversely affect contacts with neighbours, calls from relatives, visits from social services personnel?

How far is an elderly person's self-esteem affected by the feeling that they are considered at risk and consequently dependent?

Is the provision of an alarm made at the expense of some other form of social service?

The Council recommends that continuing research be carried out in the area of contact and alarm systems for the elderly in Ireland and in this context welcomes the decision of the Department of Health to assess urban and rural communication networks. The Council suggests the following guidelines in the provision of communication systems by voluntary and statutory groups:

(i) Alarm/communication systems should not replace person-to-person services and contacts with the elderly person.

(ii) It should be verified that the elderly person actually wants the alarm system and is prepared to use it before it is installed.

(iii) The most appropriate and most cost effective system from the wide range currently available on the market should be selected. This will involve consultation with the elderly persons concerned.

(iv) Detailed explanation should be given to the elderly person on how the system works assuring them that confidentially will be respected.

(v) Detailed guidance for the elderly person in the technical operation of the system should be provided.

(vi) Regular servicing of systems should be carried out.

The Council endorses the Draft Standard for alarm systems for the elderly and others living at risk which has been drawn up by the European Committee for Electrotechnical Standardisation. [9]

In view of the increasing level of violence directed against the elderly, and the consequent fear and anxiety felt by many elderly persons, the Council feels that much more attention should be paid by local authorities and those implementing the Task Force on Housing Aid Scheme to security devices and locks in the designing, repairing and maintenance of houses occupied by the elderly using as much of modern technology as possible. Many such devices, such as peepholes, guard chains and safety locks for windows and doors, are relatively cheap and simple to install, while at the same time providing a reasonable level of security.

The Council also urges greater vigilance by the elderly themselves and people caring for them in relation to fire prevention. A detailed resume of how such vigilance can be exercised is given in Appendix 8 of this report. The installation of a smoke detector alarm in the homes of elderly people would be most useful in this respect.

The Council recommends that each health board should, in conjunction with the local authority and the crime prevention unit of the Garda Siochana, provide detailed information on alarm and security systems as part of a comprehensive Aids and Information Service for the Elderly in each community care area. This information should be available in a manner and at a location which is easily accessible to elderly persons, their families and voluntary groups caring for the elderly.

CHAPTER 8

IMPROVEMENT SCHEMES FOR ELDERLY DWELLINGS

House Improvement Grants

For those who can afford to have repairs or improvements carried out themselves a House Improvement Grant is available from the Department of the Environment. Grant assistance is available under the current scheme for the provision of a water supply (£200), sewage facilities (£200), the provision of a chimney (£600), the provision of a bathroom (£600), an additional bedroom to relieve overcrowding (£600) or for major necessary works to the basic fabric of the house (£600).

If the work consists of any two of the last three mentioned improvements the maximum grant payable is £1,000 and where all three jobs have to be carried out the maximum is £1,400.

Because the first three mentioned are special grants they are not affected by any other works. However, the Department stipulates that in any of the above cases the amount of grant cannot exceed two thirds of the approved cost.

The present scheme is in appropriate for many elderly persons. For instance, it is likely that many would be unable to organise such a project without assistance and, also, it is likely that many elderly persons would have difficulty in bearing the balance of the cost of improvement.

Essential Repairs Grants

An essential repairs grants scheme is operated by local authorities which is confined to houses in rural areas that cannot be made fit for human habitation in all respects at a reasonable cost.

The basic objective of the scheme is to enable a local authority to give assistance for the carrying out of minimal repairs to prolong the life of a house for the lifetime of the occupants, who are usually elderly. Such repairs enable the person/s to remain living in their own environment without the local authority having to provide new accommodation which would not be used on a long-term basis.

Local authorities are empowered to pay a grant of up to the full approved costs of the work considered necessary and they in turn, recoup half their individual grants from the Department of the Environment subject to a maximum of £300 in any one case. In some instances the local authorities are prepared to carry out the work themselves on the applicant's behalf.

Assistance under the above scheme is, however, confined to the fabric of the dwelling and it does not cover the provision of water, sewerage and other facilities.

Reconstruction Loans

A reconstruction loan is also available from the local authority. A loan of up to £1,000 may be given unsecured. For anything above £1,000 to a maximum of £6,500 security is required. The maximum income limit for applicants is £8,000 per annum. These loans are limited to 10 or 15 years. Because of the natural reluctance of elderly people to enter into debt and having to meet the cost of repayments, along with the worry of the outstanding balance, it is important that they be supported and reassured of the legal implications involved, if the loan scheme is to be used.

Task Force on Special Housing Aid for the Elderly

A special but limited programme commenced in 1982 to improve the living conditions of elderly persons living alone in unfit and unsanitary conditions in either pprivately rented or owned dwellings. A Task Force was appointed under the aegis of the Department of the Environment which included representatives of the Department, the Departments of Health and Social Welfare, local authorities and voluntary bodies to carry out this programme. The Government allocated £1 million to the scheme in 1982 with the same amount being provided for 1983 and again for 1984. The Public Capital Programme for 1985 included a further £1 million for the Task Force. This special aid programme is administered at regional level by the health boards, who may arrange for the carrying out of an approved scheme of necessary works on behalf of an elderly person who is not himself in a position to have the work carried out. The scheme applies in both rural and urban areas. There is no formal means test and the scheme provides for the payment of up to 100% of the cost of any work carried out. If a person receives assistance under this scheme they will not qualify for other improvement or repairs grants.

Typically, aid is available for necessary repairs to make a dwelling habitable for the lifetime of the occupant, repairs to a chimney or fireplace to ensure a source of heat, the provision of water and sanitary facilities, the provision of food storage facilities, works to facilitate access to a house, e.g. a ramp or handrail, etc. Where necessary the health board may arrange alter-

Table 8.1: *Monies allocated to each Health Board under the Special Task Force to improve the Living Conditions of the Elderly 1983, 1984*

Health Board	1983 Allocation £	1984 Allocation £
Eastern Health Board	137,000	155,000
Midland Health Board	117,000	110,000
Mid-Western Health Board	90,000	65,000
North-Eastern Health Board	140,000	130,000
North-Western Health Board	133,000	150,000
South-Eastern Health Board	97,000	50,000
Southern Health Board	117,000	125,000
Western Health Board	135,000	185,000

Source: *Department of the Environment, 1985.*

native accommodation for an elderly person while works are being carried out on his dwelling.

The scheme is seen essentially as a flexible and efficient means of providing necessary repairs to the dwellings of elderly persons living alone in the community. Thus it is administered by the health boards who have close contact with the elderly through the community care system. The annual allocation for each area is based primarily on the proportion of elderly in the health board region, relative poverty indicators such as the condition of dwellings as identified from the Census of Population and the demand generally for the scheme.

Each health board has formed an ad hoc committee, representative of the health board, the local authority, voluntary bodies and AnCO if they are participating in the carrying out of work under the scheme.

In most of the health board areas the Task Force is operated on a community care basis with each community care area having its own steering committee. The work is carried out by voluntary organisations, contractors and where practical by AnCO trainees under the direction of designated foremen. The level of involvement by local authorities in the scheme varies from health board to health board and from county to county. In some instances, local authorities appear to be very involved in the scheme, in others they are not so involved. It is estimated that over 3,500 homes of the elderly have been repaired under the scheme, ranging from small jobs to larger ones of roof repairs and installation of sanitary and water facilities. However, the installation of septic tanks and the sinking of wells has been left in abeyance in many cases because of the considerable investment of funds required in an individual case. Apart from the general objectives set out in its terms of reference the Task Force has not set down specific guidelines for the types of work to be carried out or on the way the money allocated to each health board area is to be spent. Yet, some health boards apply an upper limit on the amount of money to be spent on any one job. This means that in such areas the provision of water and sewerage facilities has not been undertaken. Generally, the emphasis has been on urgent repair works which have been seen as a first priority. While there are indications that water and sanitary installations are now being undertaken in areas where this was not the case up to now, there remain areas where this work is not being carried out. In this respect, the Council regrets the failure of the Task Force to deal with major structural repairs and installations that are necessary in many instances, particularly in remote rural areas.

Figures available to the Council suggest that applications under the Task Force scheme have been much greater than the number of jobs carried out, though account must be taken of the fact that many of these applicants would not be eligible. With current rates of progress, it is likely to take three years to complete the work already referred and approved.

The waiting list which has developed as a result of the huge number of approved applications appears, in the Council's view, to militate against what was felt to be the major strength of the scheme, that is, a flexible and efficient means of providing basic repairs to the fabric of houses of elderly people in need.

The Council recommends:

1. That provision for house improvements for the elderly currently being made under the Task Force scheme be established on a long term basis, with the provision of extra funding as necessary.

2. That the Department of the Environment set up a separate grant scheme to cater for the major structural repairs and installations, (i.e. water, septic tank), necessary to provide basic amenities in dwellings of elderly persons in both rural and urban areas. Such a scheme would be an extension of the present Essential Repairs Grant Scheme and should provide for grant-aid of up to 100% of the repair and installation costs.

The Council recognises that some essential repair work cannot be undertaken under the Task Force Scheme because of the refusal of the occupant of a house to co-operate with any outside agency — voluntary or statutory. This raises important, complex and sensitive ethical questions which must be addressed by all those involved in the provision of services to the elderly.

CHAPTER 9

SELECTED POLICY IMPLICATIONS AND HOUSING OPTIONS

The Elderly Living Alone

The relatively high numbers of elderly people in the single and widowed category and the growing proportion of these living alone makes certain demands on health and social services, including housing provision.

Single or widowed persons, particularly, if living alone, are probably more likely to neglect themselves than their married peers and so to a greater extent require institutional provision for their care. Binchy and Walsh[1] found that, among admissions of those aged 65 years and over to geriatric and psychiatric facilities in one catchment area, those having a living spouse constituted less than one-third of geriatric admissions and less than one-quarter of psychiatric admissions. The Department of Health[2] survey of persons in long-stay geriatric institutions in 1975 showed that 40% of such persons would otherwise live alone. The following table (Table 9.1) compares the marital status of the elderly population in general with that of elderly persons in geriatric institutions.

The predominant reason for living alone, given by nearly 50% of respondents in the St. Vincent de Paul Survey, is the death of a marriage partner. There were 7% who stated they were living alone because they made a personal decision to do so.

"It is so important to bear in mind that the great majority of the old and alone interviewed never made any formal choice or arrangements about living alone, although some may have chosen to remain in the situation once it was thrust upon them". [3]

Power, [4] not surprisingly, found that "lonliness afflicts two-fifths of elderly people at various levels — occasionally (25%), frequently (7%) and persistently (7%)".

The theme of loneliness and the rural elderly has been discussed in depth by Daly and O'Connor in a study carried out for the National Council for the Aged. They state that "loneliness and a lack of company remain the most

68

Table 9.1: *Percentage Distribution of Persons Aged 65 Years and over by Marital Status in Ireland, 1981 and in Geriatric Institutions, 1975*

	Male				Female			
	Single	Married	Widowed	Total	Single	Married	Widowed	Total
1981 Census (Ireland)	26.0	57.4	16.6	100	23.2	29.3	47.5	100
Survey of parients in Geriatric Institutions	67.7	11.0	21.3	100	49.7	8.7	41.6	100

Source: *Survey of Long-Stay Geriatric Patients, Department of Health, 1975, Census of Population 1981,*

69

outstanding problems of all elderly people who live alone".

The following response from a woman respondent, quoted by Daly and O'Connor, lists many of the possible difficulties faced by those living alone.

"The loneliness (was the biggest difference). No-one to talk to at night times. And getting grub also, cooking a bit there for yourself has no pleasure in it. When my brother was here I cooked for two and I did all my own baking on the open fire. I have never baked' a cake since he died. I buy bread now. Sure it would only be thrown out anyway as I wouldn't use it. I was always noted for having the unusual apple tart (but not now). [6]

Power makes the point that if one basic reason for loneliness among the old and alone can be identified 'it is quite simply lack of company'.[7]

For the elderly living alone in a large house with a number of unused rooms, the idea of sharing their dwelling with another elderly person might be welcome. This has already been seen to be suitable in some areas and indeed, would combat many of the problems encountered through lack of human contact.

It is worth noting that about 23% of single households found their accommodation 'too big" compared with only 4% of 'other' types of households. [8] While this suggested that there may be some scope for reallocating housing among households, Whelan and Vaughan found that further analysis of the data in the ESRI survey suggested that this scope was extremely limited. The vast majority of those who considered their present accommodation 'rather too big" replied 'no' when asked whether they would like to move house. [9] Thus, according to Whelan and Vaughan, their dissatisfaction with their dwelling does not seem to be sufficiently strong to enourage them to think of moving and, hence, the idea of re-allocating housing from elderly households to younger, larger families is unlikely to find widespread acceptance. However, Whelan and Vaughan recommend that further research be undertaken on this topic which would concentrate on establishing the full range of costs (financial, social and psychological which seem to prevent elderly households from moving to smaller dwellings. [10] The Council endorses this view and recommends that such research be undertaken by the Department of the Environment.

House-sharing by Elderly People

A number of schemes have been developed in Britain and elsewhere in Europe involving house-sharing by elderly people. This may be on the basis of conversion of a house owned by one elderly person into a number of apartments, one of which is reserved for the original owner. The other apartments are occupied by other elderly persons. It may also be on the basis of the acquisition of a house on behalf of a number of elderly persons who have expressed

70

a desire to move into such accommodation. The Abbeyfield Society, which has been operating since 1956 in Britain and Northern Ireland in providing such houses for the elderly, has recently been established in Ireland and has opened a house in Dublin catering for six elderly persons (see Appendix 5). The Council wholeheartedly welcomes this and other similar developments. For example, 'Homestay' operates as a non-profit making organisation in Dublin to help the active elderly to cope with the twin problems of accommodation in a non-institutionalised home-from-home environment and loneliness. It puts those with accommodation to offer in touch with those elderly seeking accommodation. 'Homestay' also offers day residency during the week for elderly persons requiring such accommodation.

The lifestyle of residents in group housing varies from relatively complete independence in homes where residents carry out all aspects of home management, to more supportive environments where the sponsoring agency provides varying levels of managerial and social services. Abbeyfield, for example, has found it necessary to develop "extra care" units for those residents needing some nursing care after perhaps years of living more independently in a typical Abbeyfield Home.

Leasehold Schemes for the Elderly

In Britain, the National Federation of Housing Associations has devised Leasehold Schemes for the Elderly (see Appendix 6). These are sponsored by the Department of the Environment and the Housing Corporation (the state body charged with the development and funding of co-operative housing). These schemes enable owners to dispose of their existing property and lease more suitable accommodation at a subsidised rate. The total cost of each scheme is covered by the sum of the premium paid by elderly persons for the leases plus grants.

The purpose of statutory grants is to ensure that the price of the leasehold can be within the means of owners of rather ordinary properties and to facilitate the provision of warden accommodation and some common facilities within the price. Any surplus from the sale of their present home, after re-investing in a leasehold scheme, will help towards the financial independence and maintenance of a reasonable standard of living by the elderly person.

The Housing Association retains management responsibility for the scheme, including warden service, maintenance and repair, and maintaining a list of potential leaseholders. The lease reverts to the Association at the end of the leaseholders occupation.

The Council believes that the development of similar schemes in Ireland would be extremely beneficial in that they would offer another alternative to elderly persons who are owner-occupiers and find their accommodation

71

too big or too isolated. The uptake of such schemes by elderly persons would also free larger properties for use by younger families and thereby make for more efficient use of existing housing stock. The Council recommends that the Department of the Environment establish two such schemes on a pilot basis in conjunction with an existing voluntary housing association or voluntary organisation interested in the welfare of the elderly.

Home Extensions
The number of elderly people living with relatives and families continues to be high despite the trend towards independent living. Given that one of the most important factors in maintaining people in the community with a reasonable degree of independence is the strength of marriage and family ties, the Council considers that it is now necessary to radically evaluate the current network of family support services with a view to providing the level of support necessary to enable the elderly to continue to live with, or in close proximity to, families and relatives.

The ESRI survey showed that there was a sharp contrast between the amount of help available to those living alone and those living with others.[11] Over 80% of persons living in multi-member households stated that another member of the household would care for them in the event of illness, and only about one in twenty said they would have to go to hospital. In contrast, almost 33% of those living alone replied that they would have to go to hospital.

The Council recognises that the bulk of care for the elderly in the community is provided by families and sees a continuing central role for the family in this respect. Housing, health and social welfare policies should support and re-inforce the family as the basic caring agency. In this respect the Council feels that there is wide scope to improve and extend existing reconstruction grant and loan schemes in order to encourage and facilitate families who wish to provide 'granny flat' type of accommodation within their own dwelling, either local authority or private, to enable the elderly grandparents to remain with the family. This type of accommodation facilitates the elderly person remaining in the community, close to his/her family, while retaining the desired level of independence. As such, it is a key factor in maintaining the elderly person in the community. It is also likely that the provision of 'granny flat' extensions will be very much less expensive than the provision of independent accommodation.

The Council considers that families wishing to maintain elderly relatives in their own homes should receive the maximum level of support, encouragement and practical aid from all relevant agencies.

The Council recommends that the Department of the Environment should set up a specific grant aid scheme for families who wish to extend their homes in order to provide self-contained independent accommodation for elderly relatives. The criteria for grant aid should be relatively strict in order to eliminate possible abuses of such a scheme.

Mortgage Annuity[12]

Currently, elderly home owners in Ireland do not have the option of converting part of the value of their dwelling into an income through a mortgage annuity. In Britain, a number of Insurance companies offer a 'home income scheme': under this, a pensioner takes out a mortgage on the house with a life company and uses the mortgage money to buy an annuity. The mortgage interest is deducted from the annuity payments, with the balance yielding the income. Under these schemes, the financial institution gives a loan which is repayable on death, with no capital repayments during the person's lifetime. The loan is used to buy a lifetime income; part of that income pays the interest on the loan. The person still owns the house. The house can be sold on the death of that person and part of the proceeds paid to the financial institution, with the rest going to the person's heirs.

Those pensioners who paid tax were able to claim tax relief on the mortgage interest. For those pensioners whose incomes were so low that they paid no tax, the scheme was of limited benefit until, in 1980, an amendment to the Housing Act gave those pensioners who paid no tax, the option of paying a lower interest charge on the mortgage (the 'option mortgage') with the life company being reimbursed by the Government. For someone aged 70 and over, a 75% mortgage on a house valued at £23,000, taken out to buy an annuity, would yield after-tax income of about £1,500 per annum, at an interest rate of about 10%. In addition, any increases in the value of the home goes to the pensioners, though the annuity is not itself protected from the effects of inflation.

Alternatively, through a similar mortgage on the house, reversionary loans could be made available whereby a capital sum would be given to the elderly person rather than an annual income.

Many elderly persons in Ireland would not wish to use such a scheme, even if it were available. But some presumably would, and there would be a widening in the range of choice available to pensioners. No Government subsidy would be involved, although the tax arrangements under an 'option mortgage' would involve a relatively small amount of extra expenditure.

In view of the larger proportion of house ownership among the elderly in Ireland, the Council recommends that schemes, which enable a capital asset to be converted into income, should be developed by existing financial institutions such as building societies and insurance companies.

In this respect, an interesting suggestion has been put forward by Michael

Fogarty as follows:

> "One idea which you might like to consider for spreading this type of provision more widely is to encourage local authorities to become agents for it: there is after all no net long term cost to public funds. And nothing concentrates commefcial agencies' minds so sharply as a bit of competition." [13]

The Council also recommends that the facility of an 'option mortgage' should be considered by the Government.

Capital Acquisitions Through Inheritance

The Council believes that there is a need to review the current system of taxation in regard to capital acquisitions through inheritance. The current provisions for inheritance by people other than a spouse or child who had shared a house with a deceased person during his/her lifetime are inadequate. The survivor, who in many instances is an elderly person, may be left with a tax bill which they are unable to pay except through mortgaging the house, a prospect which many would feel quite threatening in their later years.

CHAPTER 10

CO-ORDINATING HOUSING AND OTHER COMMUNITY-BASED SERVICES

Introduction

The analysis and discussion contained in this report have shown that the housing of elderly persons is a diverse and complex subject, with many differing strands. Planners, formal carers and policy-makers are invariably not old themselves and so cannot draw on first-hand experiences. Nevertheless, the essential task and challenge for both planners and service providers remains one of responding to the private sorrows of individuals, sorrows, which regrettably still frequently go unnoticed even by those in the fore-front of caring and policy-making.

The recommendations contained in the report point towards the need for a more adequate response to the housing needs of the elderly. This chapter establishes the context with which housing programmes for the elderly can be most effectively developed.

It is the view of the Council that measures, methods and structures must be explored in order to ensure that the appropriate mix of services is provided in the community to enable more elderly people, particularly those with predominantly social problems, to be cared for in their own homes rather than in institutions. This can best be achieved if community care of elderly persons is governed by the following principles:

1. That it be seen as comprehensive, that is to say, based on informed and up-to-date demographic information, which would be the basis for adequate provision at every level and which would ensure that all elderly persons in need are reached, rather than just those who are referred for care.

2. That it be seen as an integrated range of services from the provision of simple supports for mainly comfort or preventative reasons to acute and long-term hospital care for those who require specialist medical or nursing attention.

75

3. That it be seen as the responsibility of a number of parties including the family, the public, the educational, housing and health authorities as well as the medical and nursing professions.

Need for Co-ordination

There are powerful social arguments in favour of non-institutional care of elderly persons. [1] Most elderly people cherish their independence even if this involves a certain amount of risk-taking. A key task, therefore, for policy-makers is to facilitate individuals living independently in the community. The ability of elderly persons to do so can be said to depend as much on the kind of accommodation they occupy as the support they receive. It is almost self-evident that poor or inappropriate housing amplifies the problems caused by handicap and failing physical powers. Environmental factors such as poor access from the street or roadway, absence of an inside lavatory, awkward staircases, inadequate heating and insulation, poorly desiged kitchens and bathrooms and too large a house can, in the presence of frailty and ill health, undermine the ability of the elderly person to cope.

The increasing numbers of elderly people in the community and particularly the growing numbers of those aged 75 years and over represents a major social challenge and presents a major test to the idea of care in the community. If this challenge is to be met, there is a need for a much greater level of flexibility and co-ordination in the provision of services — housing, social and medical — than is currently the case. The emphasis on maintaining old people in the community and in their own homes rather than in hostels or institutions requires that different agencies work together towards this end. This requires an integrated and co-ordinated approach both at the level of provision and the level of planning between:
(i)   families, voluntary groups and statutory services;
(ii) hospitals and community care services;
(iii) housing and health authorities.

The needs of elderly persons rarely fall into water-tight compartments to be met by one authority or one service only. An elderly person may be enabled to remain living in the community not only through the efforts and support of family and relatives, but also through (a) the efforts of the voluntary and neighbourhood caring network, (b) the provision of domiciliary help and care by the community services, (c) the availability of an effective rehabilitation programme and other day hospital services and (d) the efforts of the housing authority (for example improvements to, adaptation or extension of existing homes). The purposeful and smooth functioning of all these elements requires effective co-ordination at community level. This co-ordination is governed by the following considerations:

(i) The commitment of health boards to promote and facilitate the development of co-ordinated community care at the local level is an essential requirement of such care. This is because, in the first instance, it must necessarily implicate the hospital and community care programmes of the health boards. Resources may have to be redistributed, the hospital programme may have to become less insular and more community conscious and both programmes must establish a mechanism for co-ordinating their information and activities.

(ii) Appropriate and adequate accommodation is fundamental to the care of the elderly in the community. The local authority must therefore be involved in any co-ordinating mechanism established in a local community to promote improved community care provision for the elderly.

(iii) Though it may not always be adverted to, community care, by definition, implies that the people being cared for continue to live at home or in a surrogate 'home'. Community care is therefore founded on informal care, whether that be the care provided by families, by friends and neighbours or by members of voluntary organisations. The voluntary sector must necessarily be included in mechanisms designed to improve the co-ordination of the different parties to the care programme.

Thus, statutory services, whether housing, social ,or health, should (i) support and facilitate the family as the basic caring agency for elderly persons, in so far as this is appropriate and practicable, (ii) involve the voluntary sector in the provision of services where this is feasible and where the voluntary sector can augment the care provided by both the family network and the statutory services.

The Council recommends that the Department of Health set up two pilot projects which would develop and evaluate the concept of co-ordination of services for the elderly at the level of both planning and provision at local level. Such projects would be located in selected community care areas which are generally co-terminous with local authority functional areas and would ideally have a rural and an urban dimesnion. The projects would seek to involve all contributors to the caring network, family, voluntary, statutory; health and housing authorities; hospital and community care programmes. All should participate in the development of an appropriate co-ordinated community-based range of care of care for elderly persons.

The Council wishes to stress that while co-ordination is not a substitute for adequate resources, it may, nevertheless, help to ensure that what resources are available are used to the best effect, and so limit duplication and waste.

Health and Housing Authorities

The inter-relatedness of an elderly person's needs suggests a high measure of common interest between health and housing authorities. At a minimum level, co-ordination between the two authorities represents a recognition of common interests which in turn calls for a willingness to share knowledge and engage in consultation. Commentating on the situation in England, Hearnden states that "without a change of attitude, significant improvements are unlikely to occur". [2] Bytheway and James point to a "considerable and fundamental difference" [3] in belief and attitude between housing and social services officers. Such differences of perspective can give rise on both sides to exaggerated and dysfunctional stereotypes and images of each others' role. For example, according to one study social workers were seen as 'blue-jean philanthropists' and housing officers as 'insensitive and geared to dealing with units, not people. [4] It would appear that as a basic starting point there is a need for more information and more understanding about the roles and constraints of the different personnel and different agencies. This requires, first of all, an identification and recognition of a common interest, i.e. the maintenance and support of elderly persons in the community, between health and housing authorities and their respective personnel.

Such a common interest leads to a sharing of knowledge and information which is the "nitty-gritty of co-ordination" [5] and which should result in some measure of joint action. In many instances such sharing of information occurs on an informal and ad hoc basis and thus influences the actions of some of the personnel involved. Some local authorities in Britain have gone beyond such ad hoc arrangements between individuals and have set up joint care co-ordination teams or their equivalent to discuss policy and plans relating to the elderly and pool relevant information. Such teams were felt by Hearnden to lead to 'more productive dialogue' [6] than the more informal and ad hoc arrangements between individuals that operated in many authorities.

In 1976 Stockport local authority produced a jointly agreed overall strategy between housing and social services departments for the longer-term development of services to meet the needs of its elderly population. [7] In essence this implied a considerable shift away from 'residential' solutions to support for the elderly in their own homes and a consequent shift of resources.

The need for co-ordination between health and housing authorities in the Irish context is obvious. With a view to facilitating such co-ordination the Council recommends that each local authority and each health board should designate an officer or officers to be responsible for liaison in matters concerning the elderly. Initially, where staffing numbers do not allow, this might need to be part of a wider brief. Such officers should be of senior rank and would have responsibility for such matters as joint planning, information sharing, joint financial allocations where appropriate (e.g. sheltered housing) and joint in-service training for selected staff of both agencies.

CHAPTER 11

SUMMARY OF RECOMMENDATIONS

Introduction

The Council, on the basis of its consideration of the issue of housing and the elderly in Ireland, wishes to make a number of recommendations which are summarised in this chapter under the following headings:

1. Local Authorities.
2. Voluntary Housing Associations.
3. Sheltered Housing.
4. Private Rented Accommodation.
5. Alarm/Communication Systems.
6. Task Force on Special Housing Aid for the Elderly.
7. Elderly Owner-Occupiers.
8. Caring for the Elderly at Home.
9. Co-ordination of Services for the Elderly at Local Level.
10. Health and Housing Authorities.

Local Authorities (Chapter 3)

Since 1972 local authorities have generally allocated 10% of all new local authority dwellings to the elderly in accordance with a recommendation of the 1968 *Care of the Aged* report. Some of these old person's dwellings have been built as sheltered housing schemes and many have alarm/communication systems installed. About 20% of such dwellings are of the demountable, chalet variety.

The crucial importance of suitable housing in the maintenance of elderly people in the community and outside institutions should be taken into account in the future provision and allocation of housing, in terms of design, location and numbers of units. The 10% allocation for the elderly which has become the norm for most local authorities may be inadequate in some instances.

Recommendation 1

The Council recommends that a more wide-ranging system of allocation than currently exists should be adopted by local authorities in relation to the letting of houses to the elderly. Such a system should incorporate not only factors of overcrowding and unfitness, but also significant social, medical and environmental factors, such as:

1. *age with special reference to those aged 75 years and over;*
2. *circumstances relating to living alone and/or isolation;*
3. *suitability for housing, following appropriate assessment, of persons already in long-stay residential institutions;*
4. *homelessness, or being forced to reside in hostels, night shelters or lodging houses because of no other place to go;*
5. *the position of elderly people who are evicted from private rented accommodation because of inability to pay rent;*
6. *the desirability of facilitating some isolated older people moving to villages or centres of population;*
7. *those whose medical condition is likely to be adversely affected by the unsuitability of their present accommodation;*
8. *the desirability of housing elderly persons in their own area.*

Voluntary Housing Associations (Chapter 4)

To date, voluntary associations and other voluntary groups in Ireland have provided some 1200 units of accommodation for elderly persons. While the current system of grant aid to voluntary organisations represents progress in relation to previous schemes, it is likely that the development and expansion of voluntary housing in Ireland will continue to be inhibited by inadequate or ad hoc funding. The lack of defined subsidy schemes to cover current running costs, such as those incurred on payment of/for maintenance, insurance, welfare personnel, poses significant problems for many voluntary groups and consequently limits the potential of the voluntary sector to provide housing accommodation for the elderly.

Recommendation 2

The Council recommends that defined subsidy schemes should be established to cater for running costs of voluntary housing schemes for the elderly. Such subsidy schemes would cover:

(a) current running costs (e.g. heat, light, maintenance, insurance, caretaking) under Section 12 ('Periodic Contribution') of the 1966 Housing Act;

(b) costs pf welfare caring services (meals, home helps) under Section 65 of the Health Act 1953.

Sheltered Housing (Chapter 5)

Sheltered housing schemes for the elderly have been provided by a number of local authorities, health boards, voluntary groups and private developers. In the future much greater emphasis should be placed on the provision of sheltered housing as a centrally important link in the provision of community services for the elderly and the consequent reduction in the numbers of elderly persons going into institutional care. In view of this emphasis on appropriately designed, staffed and located sheltered housing in the future provision of services for the elderly, further analysis is required in this area.

Recommendation 3

The Council, therefore, recommends that an Inter-Departmental Working Group should be set up in order to examine and assess the role and contribution of sheltered housing, both statutory and voluntary, in the provision of accommodation and selected services for the elderly within an Irish context and to make recommendations accordingly. This Working Group should be comprised of representatives from both the Department of Health and the Department of the Environment and should consult with local authorities, health boards and voluntary associations cutrrently providing sheltered accommodation for the elderly.

Private Rented Accommodation (Chapter 6)

In 1980, some 8% of all elderly person households were privately rented. In the case of elderly persons aged 80 years and over the percentage in privately rented accommodation was as high as 19%. The Housing (Private Rented Dwellings Act) 1982 and the Housing (Private Rented Dwellings (Amendment) Act, 1983 and the consequent establishment of the Rent Tribunal have enabled the setting up of structures to deal with the problems associated with dwellings that were subject to rent control, under the Rent Restrictions Acts 1960 to 1982. No such structures exist to cater for problems associated with rented accommodation not formerly controlled. In order to deal with this problem Threshold recommended the establishment of Private Rented Housing Boards that would regulate rents, adjudicate on rent adjustment and act as an arbitration service. It also proposed compulsory written leases, controlled deposits, the right of court appeal against eviction, standardised eviction notices and statutory minimum standard bye-laws. The Council considers that an alternative and equally acceptable approach would be to extend the existing Rent Tribunal to this sector, but with these extended terms of reference.

Recommmendation 4

The Council recommends that the Department of the Environment draw

up appropriate legislation with all due speed in order to instigate approp-
riate procedures to cater for problems associated with the noncontrolled
private rented sector.

Alarm/Communication Systems (Chapter 7)

The fear of falling ill or being attacked in their own home and of not being able to summon help is a constant pre-occupation for many elderly persons living alone. The Council recognises that there is no simple single solution to this problem. The issue is at once one of independence and one of protection for elderly people. Telephone contact and alarm systems provide a high level of emotional security for elderly persons but should be seen only as part of the entire community effort to help people living alone. There is no substitute for good neighbourhood surveillance both on a formal and informal basis. Consistent checking (e.g daily calling) by neighbours, relatives and social services personnel is the single most important element in the reduction of risk among the elderly who live alone.

The Council considers that further research should be carried out in the area of contact and alarm systems for the elderly in Ireland in order to establish the most appropriate and cost effective systems in the Irish context. The Council strongly supports the decision of the Department of Health to fund research on communication networks in urban and rural areas.

Recommendation 5

The Council recommends that each health board should, in conjunction with the local authority and the crime prevention unit of the Garda Siochana, provide detailed information on alarm and security systems as part of a comprehensive aids and information system for the elderly in each community care area. This information should be available in a manner and at a location which is easily accessible to elderly persons, their families and voluntary groups caring for the elderly.

Task Force on Special Housing Aid for the Elderly (Chapter 8)

A special but limited programme commenced in 1982 to improve the living conditions of elderly persons living alone in unfit and unsuitable conditions in either privately rented or privately owned dwellings. Since 1982, the Government has allocated £1 million to the scheme each year. The scheme operates under the aegis of the Department of the Environment but is administered by the regional health boards. It is seen essentially as a flexible and efficient means of providing necessary repairs to the dwellings of elderly persons.

It is estimated that over 3,500 homes of the elderly have been repaired under the aegis of the Department of the Environment but is administered repairs and installation of water and sanitary facilities. However, in many instances larger repair jobs and the installation of septic tanks and the sinking of wells have been left in abeyance because of the considerable investment of funds required in an individual case. Currently, there is a long waiting list of work already referred and approved and it has been estimated that with current rates of progress it will take three years to carry out all such work.

Recommendation 6
The Council recommends that provision for house improvements for the elderly currently being made under the Task Force scheme be established on a long term basis, with the provision of extra funding, as necessary.

Recommendation 7
The Council also recommends that the Department of the Environment set up a separate grant scheme to cater for the major structural repairs and installations, i.e. water, septic tank, necessary to provide basic amenities in dwellings of elderly persons in both rural and urban areas. Such a scheme would be an extension of the present Essential Repairs Grant Scheme and should provide for grant-aid of up to 100% of the repair and installation costs.

Elderly Owner-Occupiers (Chapter 9)
In 1980, some 67% of elderly persons in Ireland owned their dwellings outright with a further 15% having mortgages or tenant purchase schemes. In some cases ownership may be a liability for the less active or less prosperous elderly person. He or she may lack the skill, initiative, financial resources or the physical capacity to undertake the necessary repairs and maintenance or to provide adequate heating in bigger and frequently run down older houses.

For the elderly living alone in a large house with a number of unused rooms, the idea of moving house or sharing their dwelling with another elderly person may be desirable. A number of schemes have been developed in Britain and elsewhere in Europe involving house sharing by elderly people. This may be on the basis of conversion of the house owned by an elderly person into a number of apartments, one of which is reserved for the original owner. It may also be on the basis of the acquisition of a house on behalf of a number of elderly persons who have expressed a desire to move into such accommodation. A number of schemes in Britain, sponsored by the Department of the Environment and the Housing Corporation, enable elderly owners to dispose of their existing property and lease more suitable accomodation at a subsidised rate. An ESRI study found that the vast majority of elderly persons in Ireland who found their present accommodation 'rather too big' replied 'no' when asked whether they would like to move house.

Recommendation 8

The ESRI Report recommends that further research be undertaken which would concentrate on establishing the full range of costs (financial, social and psychological) which seem to prevent elderly households from moving to smaller dwellings. The Council endorses this view and recommends that such research be undertaken by the Department of the Environment.

The Council believes that the development of schemes in Ireland which would facilitate house moving and/or house sharing would be extremely beneficial in that they would offer another alternative to elderly persons who are owner-occupiers and find their accommodation too big or too isolated. The uptake of such schemes by elderly persons would also free larger properties for use by younger families and thereby make for more efficient use of existing housing stock.

Recommendation 9

The Council recommends that the Department of the Environment establish two schemes which would facilitate house moving and/or house sharing by elderly persons, on a pilot basis, in conjunction with an existing voluntary housing association or voluntary organisation interested in the welfare of the elderly.

Currently, elderly home owners in Ireland do not have the option, which is open to their peers in Britain, of converting part of the value of their dwelling into an income which, in some instances, they require for health or other purposes.

Recommendation 10

The Council recommends that mortgage annuity schemes, which enable a capital asset to be converted into an income or capital sum, should be developed by existing financial institutions such as building societies and insurance companies. The Council also recommends that the facility of an 'option mortgage', whereby persons who paid no tax would have the option of paying a lower interest charge on the mortgage, should be considered by the Government who would reimburse the financial institution accordingly.

Caring for the Elderly at Home (Chapter 9)

The Council recognises that the greater part of care for the elderly in the community is provided by families and sees a continuing central role for the family in this respect. Housing, health and scoial welfare policies should support and re-inforce the family as the basic caring agency. In this respect, the Council feels that there is wide scope to improve and extend existing reconstruction grant and loan schemes in order to encourage and facilitate families who wish to provide 'granny flat' type accommodation within their own dwelling, either local authority or private, to enable the elderly grand-parents to remain with the family. This type of accommodation facilitates the elderly person remaining in the community, close to his/her family, while retaining the desired level of independence. As such, it is a key factor in maintaining the elderly person in the community.

Recommendation 11
The Council recommends that the Department of the Environment should set up an additional specific grant aid scheme for families who wish to extend their homes in order to provide self-contained independent accommodation for elderly relatives. The criteria for grant aid should be relatively strict in order to eliminate possible abuse of such a scheme.

Co-Ordinating Services for the Elderly at Local Level (Chapter 10)
The needs of elderly persons rarely fall into water-tight compartments to be met by one authority or one service only. An elderly person may be enabled to remain living in the community, not only through the efforts and support of family and relatives, but also through (a) the efforts of the voluntary caring network, (b) the provision of domiciliarly help and care by community services, (c) the availability of an effective rehabilitation programme and other day hospital services and (d) the efforts of the housing authority (e.g. improvements, adaption or extension of existing homes). The purpose-ful and smooth functioning of all of these elements requires effective co-ordination at community level.

Recommendation 12
The Council recommends that the Department of Health set up two pilot projects which would develop and evaluate the concept of co-ordination of services for the elderly at the level of both planning and provision at local level. Such projects would be located in selected community care areas which are generally co-terminous with local authority functional areas and would ideal-ly have a rural and an urban dimension. The projects would seek to involve all contributors to the caring network, family, voluntary, statutory; health and housing authorities; hospital and community care programmes. All should participate in the development of an appropriate co-ordinated community-based range of care for elderly persons.

Health and Housing Authorities (Chapter 10)
The inter-relatedness of an elderly person's needs suggests a high measure of common interest between health and housing authorities. At a minimum co-ordination between the two authorities represents a recognition of comm-on interests which in turn calls for a willingness to share knowledge and en-

86

gage in consultation.

There is a need for more information and more understanding about the roles and constraints of the different personnel and different agencies. This requires, first of all, an identification and recognition of a common interest, i.e. the maintenance and support of elderly persons in the community, between health and housing authorities and their respective personnel.

Recommendation 13

The Council recommends that each local authority and each health board should designate an officer to be responsible for liaison in designing structures and services to maintain and support elderly people in the community. Initially where staffing numbers do not allow, this might need to be part of a wider brief. Such officers should be of senior rank and would have responsibility for such matters as joint planning, information sharing, joint financial allocation where appropriate (e.g. sheltered housing) and joint in-service training for selected staff of both agencies.

REFERENCES

Introduction
(1) Central Policy Review Staff, *Population and the Social Services* HMSO, 1977.

Chapter 1

(1) *Census of Population 1981,* Volume 2, Central Statistics Office, Dublin.
(2) National Council for the Aged, *Incomes of the Elderly in Ireland: And An Analysis of the State's Contribution,* 1984, p. 33.
(3) *Census of Population 1981,* Volume 3. Central Statistics Office, Dublin.
(4) For a more detailed analysis of these projections, see *Appendix 2.*

Chapter 2

(1) NESC Report No. 69, *Housing Requirements and Population Change,* Dublin, 1983.
(2) Wicks, W., "Community Care and Elderly People" in Walker, A., (Ed.), *Community Care, The Family, The State and Social Policy,* Blackwell and Robertson, Oxford, 1982, p. 102.
(3) *Report on Survey in North Leitrim,* North Leitrim Care of the Aged Committees, 1985.
(4) Department of the Environment, *National Dwelling and Housing Survey,* HMSO, 1978.
(5) Whelan, B.J, and Vaughan R.N., *The Economic and Social Circumstances of the Elderly,* ESRI, Paper 110, 1982, p. 71.
(6) Power, B., *Old and Alone in Ireland,* Society of St. Vincent de Paul, 1980, p. 13.
(7) *Census of Population 1981,* Volume 3, Central Statistics Office, Dublin.
(8) *The Human Settlements Situation and Related Trends and Policies,* Department of the Environment Monograph, 1983, p.29.

(9) *Census of Population 1981, Five Per Cent Sample Estimates, Housing and Households,* Central Statistics Office, Dublin.

(10)*Ibid.*

(11)Gilligan, R. in Kennedy S. (ed.), *One Million Poor?* Turoe Press, 1981 p. 121.

(12)Whelan, B.J. and Vaughan, R.N., *op. cit.,* p. 73.

(13)Martin, J.L. and Doyle, V.G., "Survey of the Elderly in an Urban General Practice", *Irish Medical Journal,* November 1984, Vol. 77, No. 11.

(14)Kelleher, C. and O'Mahony, A., *Marginalisation in Irish Agriculture,* An Foras Taluntais, 1984.

(15)*Ibid,* p. 91.

(16)Solan, J., Paper presented at a Conference, *The Elderly in Rural Areas: Issues for Policy and Practice,* held at the National Institute for Higher Education, Limerick, December 1984.

(17)*Ibid.*

(18)Power, B., *op. cit.,* p. 39.

(19)Department of the Environment, *op. cit.,* p. 29.

(20)National Council for the Aged, *op. cit.,* p. 81.

(21)*Report of a Single-Night Survey,* Simon Community, Dublin, 1984.

(22)*Report of the Joint Working Group on Homelessness,* Northern Ireland Office, August 1984.

(23)Department of the Environment, *A Home of Their Own,* HMSO, 1983.

(24)Drable, M. et al, *Single and Homeless,* HMSO, 1982.

(25)Digby, P.W., *Hostels and Lodgings for Single People,* HMSO, 1976.

Chapter 3

(1) *Housing Acts 1966 to 1984,* The Stationery Office, Dublin.

(2) *The Care of the Aged,* Report of an Inter-Departmental Committee, The Department of Health, 1968, para 5.2.

(3) *Ibid.* para 5.6.

(4) Dublin Corporation, Special Tabulation prepared for the National Council for the Aged, 1985.

(5) Department of the Environment, Special Tabulation prepared for the National Council for the Aged, 1984.

(6) Department of the Environment, *Single and Homeless,* HMSO, 1981, p. 38.

(7) See American Psychiatric Association, *The Homeless Mentally Ill,* October 1984.

(8) Simon Community, Submission to Commission on Social Welfare, 1983.

(9) Dublin Simon Community, *The Single Homeless: The Need for a Change of Heart,* Submission to the City Councillors of Dublin Corporation,

January 1984.
(10)Report of Glasgow Council for the Single Homeless, 1982, p. 11.
(11)Glasgow Council for the Single Homeless, *Homeless Men Speak for Themselves*, 1981, p. 57.
(12)Report of an Ad Hoc Committee on the Homeless, Department of Health, December, 1984.

Chapter 5

(1) Belton, P.A. *Long-Term Care for the Dependent Elderly, Irish Medical Journal*, January 1983, Vol. 76, No. 1.
(2) Townsend, P., *The Last Refuge,* Routledge and Kegan Paul, 1962,
(3) Bosenquet, N., *New Deal for the Elderly,* Fabian Tract, Fabian Society, London, 1975.
(4) Belton, P.A. *op. cit.*
(5) *Ibid.*
(6) *The Care of the Aged,* Report of an Inter-Departmental Committee, The Department of Health, 1968, para 5.7.
(7) Circular N7/73, Department of the Environment.
(8) Dublin Corporation, Special Tabulation prepared for National Council for the Aged, 1985.
(9) Butler, A., et. al, *Sheltered Housing for the Elderly: A Critical Review,* Department of Social Policy and Administration Research Monograph, The University of Leeds, 1979, p. 61.
(10)Clayton, S., "Social Need Revisited", *Journal of Social Policy,* 12, 2, p. 222.
(11)Boldy, D., "Don't Put All Your Eggs In One Basket", *Community Care,* January 27th 1983.
(12)*Ibid.*
(13)Circular N2/70, Department of the Environment.

Chapter 6

(1) *Housing (Private Rented Dwellings) (Standards) Regulations 1984,* Stationery Office, Dublin.
(2) Threshold, *Private Rented the Forgotten Sector,* 1983.
(3) *Ibid.,* p. 40.
(4) *Ibid.,* pp. 48, 51.
(5) *Ibid.,* p. 73
(6) *Ibid.,* p.102.

Chapter 7
(1) Power, B., *op. cit*, p. 27.
(2) *Ibid.*, p. 72.
(3) *Ibid.*, p. 73.
(4) *Ibid.*,
(5) Dublin Corporation, Communication with National Council for the Aged, 1985.
(6) Connolly, P., Paper delivered at a seminar, *The Elderly in Rural Areas: Issues for Policy and Practice*, held in the National Institute for Higher Education, Limerick, October, 1984.
(7) Cited in Butler, A., "Dispensed Alarm Systems for the Elderly", *Social Work Service*, No 25, January 1981, pp. 19-22.
(8) Butler, A., *op. cit*, p. 20.
(9) Copies of this draft Standard may be obtained from the National Council for the Aged.

Chapter 9
(1) Binchy, R. and Walsh, D., "A Comparison of Consecutive Admissions to Psychiatric and Geriatric Facilities", *Irish Journal of Psychiatry*, Autumn, 1983.
(2) Department of Health, *Survey of Long-Stay Geriatric Patients*, 1975.
(3) Power B., *op. cit.*, p. 57.
(4) *Ibid.*, p. 101.
(5) Daly, M. and O'Connor, J., *The World of the Elderly: The Rural Experience*, National Council for the Aged, 1984, p. 66.
(6) *Ibid.* p. 58.
(7) Power, B., *op cit.*, p. 108.
(8) Whelan, B.J. and Vaughan, R.N. *op. cit.*, p. 73.
(9) *Ibid.*
(10) *Ibid.*
(11) *Ibid.*, p. 91.
(12) For a fuller discussion of this topic see *Incomes of the Elderly in Ireland: And An Analysis of the States Contribution*, National Council for the Aged, 1984.
(13) Fogarty, M., paper delivered at seminar, *"Incomes of the Elderly in Ireland"*, organised by the National Council for the Aged, February 1984.

Chapter 10
(1) See in particular, Townsend, P., *op. cit.*
(2) Hearnden, D., *Co-ordinating Housing and Social Services*, Centre for

Policy on Ageing, London 1984.
(3) Bytheway, B. and Jones, L., *The Allocation of Sheltered Housing: A Study of Theory, Practice and Liaison*, Medical Sociology Research Centre, University of Swansea, 1978.
(4) Hearnden, D., *op. cit.*
(5) *Ibid.*
(6) *Ibid.* p. 6.
(7) *Ibid.* p. 14.

Appendix 1

TABLES RELATING TO DEMOGRAPHIC CONSIDERATIONS

Table 1: *Population Aged 65 and Over by Sex, 1966-1981*
In parenthesis is proportion of total population

Age group	1966	1971	1979	1981	% change 1966-71	% change 1971-81
Men						
65 and over	149,949 (10.3)	150,637 (10.1)	162,968 (9.6)	165,183 (9.6)	4.6	9.7
75 and over	52,660 (3.6)	51,551 (3.4)	52,172 (3.1)	52,497 (3.1)	−2.1	1.8
80 and over	23,916 (1.7)	23,777 (1.6)	23,032 (1.4)	23,325 (1.3)	−0.6	1.9
Women						
65 and over	173,059 (12.1)	179,182 (12.1)	198,407 (11.8)	203,771 (11.9)	3.5	13.7
75 and over	66,022 (4.6)	67,531 (4.6)	77,132 (4.6)	79,400 (4.9)	2.3	17.7
80 and over	31,965 (2.2)	33,530 (2.3)	37,416 (2.2)	40,121 (2.3)	4.9	19.7
All persons						
65 and over	323,007 (11.2)	329,819 (11.1)	361,375 (10.7)	368,954 (10.7)	2.1	11.9
75 and over	118,682 (4.1)	119,082 (4.0)	129,304 (3.8)	131,897 (3.8)	0.3	10.8
80 and over	55,881 (1.9)	57,307 (1.9)	60,448 (1.8)	63,446 (1.8)	2.6	10.7

Source: Incomes of the Elderly in Ireland: And An Analysis of the State's Contribution, National Council for the Aged, Dublin, 1984.

Table 2: *Population Aged 65 and Over by Sex and Marital Status, 1966-1981*
In parenthesis is proportion of total population aged 65 and over (or aged 75 and over)

| | Aged 65 and over | | | Aged 75 and over | | |
	1966	1971	1981	1966	1971	1981
Men						
Single	40,193 (26.8)	40,315 (26.8)	42,995 (26.0)	13,466 (25.6)	12,956 (25.1)	13,185 (25.1)
Married	80,550 (53.7)	82,467 (54.7)	94,485 (57.4)	23,286 (44.2)	23,467 (45.5)	24,897 (47.4)
Widowed	29,206 (19.5)	27,855 (18.5)	27,343 (16.6)	15,908 (30.2)	15,128 (29.3)	14,415 (27.5)
Women						
Single	42,945 (24.8)	44,891 (25.1)	47,247 (23.2)	15,804 (23.9)	16,695 (24.7)	19,641 (24.7)
Married	48,953 (28.2)	50,264 (28.1)	59,647 (29.3)	10,905 (16.5)	10,917 (16.2)	11,842 (14.9)
Widowed	81,160 (46.9)	84,027 (46.9)	96,877 (47.5)	39,313 (59.5)	39,919 (59.1)	47,917 (60.3)
All persons						
Single	83,138 (27.7)	85,206 (25.8)	90,242 (24.5)	29,270 (24.7)	29,651 (24.9)	32,826 (24.9)
Married	129,503 (40.1)	132,731 (40.2)	154,492 (41.9)	34,191 (28.8)	34,384 (28.9)	36,739 (27.8)
Widowed	110,366 (34.2)	111,882 (33.9)	124,220 (33.7)	55,221 (46.5)	55,047 (46.2)	62,332 (47.3)

Source: Incomes of the Elderly in Ireland: And An Analysis of the State's Contribuiton, National Council for the Aged, Dublin, 1984.

Table 3: *Life Expectancy: Life Expectancy at selected ages for EEC countries*

Country	Period	Sex	Life expectancy in years of age				Excess of female life expectancy over male expectancy at age 0
			0	1	40	65	
Belgium	1972–76	M	68.60	68.94	32.03	12.27	6.46
		F	75.06	75.21	37.45	15.74	
Denmark	1981–82	M	71.4	71.0	33.8	13.8	6.0
		F	77.4	77.0	39.0	17.7	
France	1982	M	70.7	70.5	33.7	14.3	8.1
		F	78.8	78.5	40.7	18.5	
German Federal Republic ...	1979–81	M	69.90	69.91	32.94	13.00	6.69
		F	76.59	76.44	38.60	16.63	
Greece	1970	M	70.13	72.16	35.14	13.87	3.51
		F	73.64	75.32	37.77	15.29	
Ireland*	1978–80	M	69.47	69.48	32.23	12.38	5.48
		F	74.95	74.82	36.81	15.40	
Italy	1974–77	M	69.69	70.30	33.05	13.17	6.22
		F	75.91	76.31	38.35	16.28	
Luxembourg	1976–78	M	68.0	67.9	31.3	12.0	7.1
		F	75.1	75.0	37.1	15.5	
Netherlands	1981	M	72.7	72.4	34.8	14.0	6.6
		F	79.3	78.9	40.8	18.5	
United Kingdom ...	1977–79	M	70.0	70.0	32.6	12.6	6.2
		F	76.2	76.1	38.1	16.6	

Source: Department of Health, *Statistical Information Relevant to the Health Services,* 1984, Table A.7.

95

Table 4: *Proportion of Elderly Persons who are Heads of Household, by Sex and Marital Status, 1971, 1979*

	Male		Female		All persons	
	1971	1979	1971	1979	1971	1979
Single	50.9	53.0	36.9	39.2	43.9	45.8
Married	89.8	91.5	5.8	6.4	48.0	59.1
Widowed	65.2	68.6	59.2	66.8	60.7	67.2

Source: Incomes of the Elderly in Ireland: And An Analysis of the State's Contribution. National Council for the Aged, Dublin, 1984.

Appendix I

Table 5: *Population Projections for those Aged 65 years and over, by County and County Borough 1986, 1991, 1996, 2001, 2006*

	1981 (actual)	1986	1991	1996	2001	2006	% Change 1981 -2006
	In parenthesis in percentage of total area Population 000's						
State	369.0 (10.7)	381.0 (10.6)	387.0 (10.6)	387.0 (10.5)	385.8 (10.4)	396.4 (10.4)	7.4
Donegal	17.5 (14.0)	17.6 (13.5)	17.2 (12.8)	16.5 (12.1)	15.8 (11.5)	16.0 (11.3)	−8.6
Leitrim	4.9 (17.6)	4.8 (18.0)	4.5 (17.9)	4.1 (17.6)	3.7 (17.3)	3.4 (17.2)	−31.0
Sligo	7.9 (14.2)	7.9 (14.0)	7.8 (13.7)	7.6 (13.3)	7.1 (12.7)	7.1 (12.4)	−10.1
Galway	21.5 (12.5)	22.0 (12.4)	21.8 (12.1)	21.3 (11.7)	20.8 (11.5)	21.3 (11.5)	−0.9
Mayo	18.2 (15.9)	18.5 (16.1)	17.8 (15.9)	16.6 (15.5)	15.5 (15.1)	14.9 (14.8)	−18.1
Clare	10.9 (12.4)	11.0 (11.9)	10.9 (11.4)	10.6 (10.9)	10.3 (10.5)	10.6 (10.4)	−2.7
Limerick Co. Borough	5.5 (9.1)	5.6 (9.4)	5.9 (10.1)	6.0 (10.7)	6.0 (11.4)	6.1 (12.0)	10.9
Limerick County	10.8 (10.7)	11.2 (10.5)	11.3 (10.3)	11.1 (9.9)	11.0 (9.6)	11.5 (9.7)	6.5
Tipperary N.R.	7.0 (11.9)	7.1 (12.1)	7.3 (12.8)	7.1 (13.0)	7.0 (13.3)	6.7 (13.1)	−4.2
Cork Co. Borough	13.6 (10.0)	13.9 (10.4)	14.3 (11.0)	14.5 (11.6)	14.9 (12.5)	15.2 (13.3)	11.8
Cork	30.9 (11.6)	31.8 (11.3)	31.8 (11.0)	31.0 (10.5)	30.4 (10.1)	30.9 (10.0)	0.0
Kerry	17.2 (14.0)	17.6 (14.2)	17.1 (13.9)	16.2 (13.5)	15.3 (13.1)	15.0 (12.9)	−12.8
Carlow	3.9 (9.8)	4.0 (9.7)	4.1 (9.9)	4.1 (10.0)	4.1 (10.1)	4.2 (10.2)	7.7
Kilkenny	7.7 (10.9)	8.1 (10.8)	8.2 (10.7)	8.1 (10.4)	8.0 (10.1)	8.0 (9.9)	3.9
Tipperary S.R.	8.6 (11.3)	8.8 (11.3)	8.9 (11.5)	8.7 (11.4)	8.4 (11.1)	8.2 (10.9)	−4.8
Waterford Co. Borough	3.5 (9.3)	3.6 (8.7)	3.8 (8.9)	4.0 (9.0)	4.4 (9.5)	4.8 (10.1)	37.1
Waterford County	5.8 (11.5)	5.8 (11.5)	5.8 (11.5)	5.6 (11.2)	5.5 (11.2)	5.4 (11.3)	−6.9
Wexford	11.2 (11.3)	11.3 (11.1)	11.4 (11.2)	11.4 (11.1)	11.3 (11.2)	11.7 (11.5)	4.5
Dublin Co. Borough	58.5 (11.1)	59.1 (12.6)	60.0 (14.7)	59.5 (17.3)	57.1 (20.7)	53.0 (26.0)	−9.4
Dun Laoghaire	7.5 (13.8)	7.5 (14.2)	7.4 (14.6)	7.4 (15.2)	7.3 (15.9)	7.2 (16.6)	−4.0
Dublin County	19.9 (4.7)	24.0 (4.6)	28.4 (4.6)	33.6 (4.7)	40.6 (5.1)	51.4 (5.6)	158.3
Kildare	7.2 (6.9)	7.9 (6.6)	8.4 (6.4)	8.7 (6.1)	9.2 (6.0)	10.5 (6.2)	45.8
Wicklow	8.4 (9.6)	8.8 (9.2)	9.2 (8.9)	9.5 (8.7)	10.0 (8.7)	10.9 (8.9)	29.8
Meath	8.3 (8.7)	8.8 (8.2)	9.3 (8.0)	9.5 (7.7)	9.7 (7.5)	10.6 (7.5)	27.7
Cavan	7.4 (13.8)	7.5 (14.2)	7.4 (14.7)	7.0 (14.8)	6.5 (14.8)	6.0 (14.4)	−18.9
Louth	8.1 (9.2)	8.8 (9.5)	9.5 (10.0)	9.5 (9.9)	9.6 (9.9)	10.0 (10.1)	23.5
Monaghan	6.3 (12.3)	6.3 (11.9)	6.2 (11.7)	6.0 (11.2)	5.7 (10.8)	5.5 (10.2)	−12.7
Laois	5.6 (11.0)	5.8 (10.9)	5.9 (11.0)	5.9 (10.8)	5.7 (10.4)	5.6 (10.1)	0.0
Longford	3.9 (12.7)	4.1 (12.9)	4.1 (13.0)	4.0 (12.8)	3.8 (12.5)	3.6 (11.9)	−7.7
Offaly	5.9 (10.2)	6.3 (10.5)	6.6 (11.0)	6.6 (11.1)	6.5 (11.1)	6.5 (11.1)	10.2
Roscommon	8.5 (15.6)	8.4 (15.5)	8.1 (15.4)	7.8 (15.3)	7.3 (14.9)	6.9 (14.3)	−18.8
Westmeath	6.4 (10.4)	6.5 (10.2)	6.8 (10.6)	6.9 (10.7)	6.8 (10.7)	6.9 (10.7)	7.8

Source: Appendix 2

97

Table 6: *Population projections for those aged 75 years and over 1986, 1991, 1996, 2001, 2006, by County and County Borough*

	1981	1986	1991	1996	2001	2006	% Change 1981–2006
	In parentheses is percentage of total area population 000's						
State	131.9 (3.8)	140.1 (3.9)	150.1 (4.1)	154.4 (4.2)	157.8 (4.2)	158.5 (4.2)	20.2
Donegal	6.5 (5.2)	6.9 (5.3)	7.3 (5.5)	7.3 (5.4)	7.0 (5.1)	6.8 (4.8)	4.6
Leitrim	1.7 (6.2)	1.7 (6.4)	1.8 (7.4)	1.8 (7.8)	1.6 (7.7)	1.5 (7.6)	−11.8
Sligo	2.9 (5.2)	3.0 (5.2)	3.2 (5.6)	3.2 (5.6)	3.1 (5.6)	3.1 (5.4)	6.9
Galway	7.9 (4.6)	8.3 (4.7)	9.1 (5.0)	9.2 (5.1)	9.0 (5.0)	8.8 (4.8)	11.4
Mayo	6.5 (5.7)	6.9 (6.0)	7.6 (6.8)	7.6 (7.0)	7.1 (6.9)	6.7 (6.6)	3.1
Clare	4.0 (4.6)	4.1 (4.4)	4.4 (4.6)	4.4 (4.5)	4.3 (4.4)	4.2 (4.2)	5.0
Limerick Co. Borough	1.9 (3.1)	2.0 (3.4)	2.2 (3.7)	2.2 (3.9)	2.3 (4.3)	2.4 (4.7)	26.3
Limerick Co.	3.6 (3.6)	3.9 (3.7)	4.3 (3.9)	4.4 (3.9)	4.4 (3.9)	4.3 (3.6)	19.4
Tipperary N.R.	2.6 (4.4)	2.7 (4.6)	2.8 (4.9)	2.8 (5.1)	3.0 (5.6)	2.9 (5.7)	11.5
Cork Co. Borough	4.9 (3.6)	5.3 (3.9)	5.5 (4.3)	5.6 (4.5)	5.8 (4.9)	6.0 (5.3)	22.4
Cork	11.0 (4.1)	11.6 (4.1)	12.5 (4.3)	12.8 (4.3)	12.7 (4.2)	12.4 (4.0)	12.7
Kerry	5.8 (4.7)	6.3 (5.1)	7.0 (5.7)	7.0 (5.8)	6.7 (5.7)	6.3 (5.4)	8.6
Carlow	1.4 (3.5)	1.5 (3.6)	1.5 (3.6)	1.6 (3.8)	1.6 (4.0)	1.7 (4.0)	21.4
Kilkenny	2.7 (3.8)	2.8 (3.8)	3.0 (3.9)	3.1 (4.0)	3.2 (4.1)	3.2 (4.0)	18.5
Tipperary S.R.	3.2 (4.2)	3.2 (4.1)	3.3 (4.3)	3.4 (4.4)	3.5 (4.7)	3.4 (4.6)	6.2
Waterford Co Borough	1.3 (3.4)	1.4 (3.4)	1.5 (3.4)	1.5 (3.4)	1.6 (3.6)	1.7 (3.6)	30.8
Waterford Co.	2.1 (4.2)	2.1 (4.0)	2.1 (4.2)	2.2 (4.4)	2.2 (4.5)	2.1 (4.3)	0.0
Wexford	4.2 (4.2)	4.5 (4.4)	4.5 (4.4)	4.5 (4.5)	4.7 (4.6)	4.7 (4.6)	11.9
Dublin Co. Borough	21.0 (4.0)	22.2 (4.7)	23.1 (5.6)	23.0 (6.7)	23.7 (8.6)	23.7 (11.6)	12.9
Dun Laoghaire	2.9 (5.3)	3.2 (6.0)	3.2 (6.3)	3.1 (6.5)	3.1 (6.9)	3.2 (7.3)	10.3
Dublin Co.	6.7 (1.6)	8.0 (1.5)	9.6 (1.5)	11.4 (1.6)	13.5 (1.7)	16.0 (1.8)	138.8
Kildare	2.3 (2.2)	2.7 (2.2)	3.0 (2.2)	3.2 (2.3)	3.5 (2.3)	3.6 (2.2)	56.5
Wicklow	3.1 (3.5)	3.4 (3.6)	3.7 (3.5)	3.8 (3.5)	4.0 (3.5)	4.2 (3.4)	35.5
Meath	2.9 (3.0)	3.0 (2.8)	3.4 (2.9)	3.6 (2.9)	3.8 (2.9)	3.9 (2.8)	34.5
Cavan	2.6 (4.8)	2.6 (4.9)	2.8 (5.6)	2.8 (6.0)	2.8 (6.3)	2.6 (6.2)	0.0
Louth	2.8 (3.2)	3.0 (3.3)	3.4 (3.5)	3.7 (3.8)	4.0 (4.2)	4.0 (4.0)	42.9
Monaghan	2.3 (4.5)	2.3 (4.4)	2.4 (4.5)	2.4 (4.5)	2.4 (4.5)	2.3 (4.3)	0.0
Laois	2.0 (3.9)	2.1 (3.9)	2.2 (4.1)	2.3 (4.2)	2.4 (4.4)	2.4 (4.2)	20.0
Longford	1.3 (4.2)	1.3 (4.2)	1.5 (4.8)	1.6 (5.1)	1.6 (5.2)	1.5 (5.0)	15.4
Offaly	2.2 (3.8)	2.2 (3.7)	2.4 (3.9)	2.5 (4.3)	2.7 (4.6)	2.7 (4.6)	22.7
Roscommon	3.1 (5.7)	3.1 (5.7)	3.3 (6.3)	3.3 (6.4)	3.1 (6.4)	3.0 (6.3)	−3.2
Westmeath	2.4 (3.9)	2.4 (3.8)	2.5 (3.9)	2.6 (4.0)	2.8 (4.3)	2.8 (4.3)	16.7

Source: *Appendix 2*

98

APPENDIX 2

Population Projections by County and Planning Region, 1981 – 2006 (Prepared for the National Council for the Aged by John Blackwell).

Assumptions

For the period up to 1991, the assumptions on mortality, nuptiality, fertility and migration, are the same as those in the CSO projections of April 1985,[1] with fertility assumptions F1 and migration assumptions M1 being chosen. For the period beyond 1991, the assumptions used are as follows.

Migration

For comparison purposes, the assumptions are of net emigration over all age groups of 5,000 per annum in 1981–86 and of 7,500 per annum in 1986–91. For 1991–96 the assumption is of 10,000 per annum net emigration and for 1996–2001 the assumption is of 15,000 per annum net emigration. For the period 2001–2006 the assumption is of zero net emigration.

Mortality

For comparison purposes the CSO assumptions are of 1981 survivorship rates for the period up to 1991. For the period beyond 1991 the assumptions are as follows: 1981 survivorship rates for the five year age groups from 0–4 upwards, except for the following. In the case of age groups 60-64 and 65-69 for males, and age groups 60-64 and upwards for females (including the open-ended group 80 and over) the annual percentage rate of change in survivorship over 1971–81 is applied to the survivorship rates of 1991 in order to derive the survivorship rates up to 2006. This means that these survivorship rates get gradually higher as one moves forward in time. In the case of births, the percentage rate of change of survivorship over 1971–81 is applied to the survivorship rates of 1991 up to 2001, with the rates for 2006 being held equal to those for 2001. This also means an improvement in survivorship for births as one moves forward. This would mean that infant mortality would be around 7 per thousand by 2001 by comparison with 10.3 in 1981.

99

Ratio of male births to the total

The ratio of the CSO report is used up to 1991; a ratio of 0.517 is used there-
after: this is the average of the 1983 and the 1984 ratios.

Nuptiality

The CSO assumptions for 1991 are used for each subsequent period.

Fertility

The CSO assumptions for 1991, assumptions F1, are used for each subsequent
period.

A note on the county projections

The projections by county are derived by a method which is essentially the
same as that described in NESC report 63 by John Blackwell and John
McGregor? There are some slight changes, as one is now dealing with data for
1971–81 in building up a picture of net internal migration, while for NESC
report 63 one had 1971–79 data.

Dublin Sub-Region

There is need for caution in interpreting the population projections for the
Dublin sub-region, which consists of three areas, Dublin County Borough,
Dun Laoghaire Borough and Dublin County (excluding Dun Laoghaire
Borough). All of the projections are on the basis of the same annual flows of
net internal migration over the projection period as over 1971–76. There has
been relatively high net (internal) outmigration from Dublin Borough and
high net (internal) inmigration into Dublin County. Much of this has been
related to housing clearance and house construction. Beyond a certain point,
the population of Dublin County Borough could be expected to stabilise at
some lower level than its currnt level. This would imply a lower rate of
increase in population in County Dublin, beyond that point. For these
reasons it is advisable to take the Dublin sub-region as a whole when considering the population projections.

1. *Population and Labour Force Projection 1986– 1991*
   Central Statistics Office, Dublin, 1985.
2. *Population and Labour Force Projections by County and Region, 1979–*
   1991, NESC Report No. 63, Dublin, 1982.

100

MALES

ESTIMATED POPULATION, 1886

COUNTIES	AGED 0-4	AGED 5-9	AGED 10-14	AGED 15-19	AGED 20-24	AGED 25-29	AGED 30-34	AGED 35-39	AGED 40-44
DONEGAL	6,366	7,341	6,857	6,155	4,675	3,804	6,180	4,218	3,781
LEITRIM	1,169	1,322	1,236	1,061	0,911	0,835	0,853	0,841	0,697
SLIGO	2,633	2,802	2,669	2,525	2,911	1,755	1,910	0,979	1,581
GALWAY	8,202		8,940	8,487	7,363	6,263	6,036	5,929	5,074
MAYO	5,142	6,017	5,742	4,011	3,805	3,198	3,718	3,833	3,224
CLARE	4,609	5,018	4,829	4,063	3,222	3,047	3,208	3,373	2,808
LIMERICK – BOR	2,701	2,557	2,034	3,006	3,019	2,737	1,900	1,698	1,423
LIMERICK – CO	4,860	5,830	5,627	4,894	3,109	3,836	4,098	3,868	3,257
TIPPERARY – NR	2,610	3,110	3,086	2,707	2,352	2,116	1,918	1,998	1,544
CORK – BOR	5,508	5,288	6,164	6,020	7,335	6,325	4,064	3,484	1,368
CORK – CO	13,548	15,456	14,607	12,582	10,004	10,007	10,430	10,224	8,164
KERRY	5,560	6,177	6,130	5,457	4,607	4,018	4,294	4,178	3,596
CARLOW	2,074	2,280	2,207	1,896	1,607	1,553	1,483	1,330	1,127
KILKENNY	3,815	3,924	3,824	3,350	2,777	2,777	2,709	2,557	2,126
TIPPERARY – SR	3,032	4,086	4,043	3,980	3,465	2,602	2,740	2,484	2,040
WATERFORD – BOR	2,004	1,932	2,007	2,113	1,808	1,466	1,313	1,204	1,118
WATERFORD – CO	2,371	2,873	2,597	2,407	1,928	1,729	1,780	1,732	1,416
WEXFORD	5,122	5,491	5,425	4,940	4,017	3,616	3,450	3,250	2,872
DUBLIN – BOR	16,325	12,342	17,718	22,344	20,129	25,638	12,125	10,673	10,505
DUN LAOIRE	2,159	1,713	2,007	2,344	2,578	2,201	1,481	1,305	1,249
DUBLIN – CO	30,495	33,070	29,186	23,645	25,101	19,483	23,481	21,667	15,957
KILDARE	6,432	7,057	6,841	5,777	5,000	4,850	5,112	4,880	3,791
WICKLOW	4,011	5,294	6,015	4,198	3,562	3,444	3,535	3,633	2,922
MEATH	5,032	6,403	6,151	2,315	3,182	3,730	1,797	4,010	3,279
CAVAN	2,401	2,886	2,570	2,315	2,102	1,933	1,797	1,701	1,410
LOUTH	4,749	4,841	4,161	4,402	3,915	3,548	3,243	2,991	2,614
MONAGHAN	2,608	3,057	2,702	2,327	2,160	1,903	1,838	1,751	1,600
LAOIS	2,788	2,995	2,702	2,660	2,286	2,001	1,878	1,634	1,443
LONGFORD	1,522	1,753	1,635	1,421	1,218	1,024	1,144	1,101	0,830
OFFALY	2,965	3,305	3,231	2,945	1,850	2,182	1,961	1,803	1,543
ROSCOMMON	2,390	2,845	2,633	2,517	1,852	1,654	1,772	1,602	1,430
WESTMEATH	3,032	3,320	3,217	3,198	2,713	2,283	2,284	2,117	1,719

REGIONS	AGED 0-4	AGED 5-9	AGED 10-14	AGED 15-19	AGED 20-24	AGED 25-29	AGED 30-34	AGED 35-39	AGED 40-44
DONEGAL	6,366	7,341	6,857	6,155	4,675	3,804	6,180	4,218	3,781
NORTHWEST	3,802	4,124	3,905	3,586	2,988	2,590	2,763	2,820	2,278
WEST	13,344	15,041	14,682	13,101	11,168	9,461	9,754	9,762	8,298
MIDWEST	11,900	16,563	16,476	14,760	12,762	11,736	11,124	10,837	9,032
SOUTHWEST	24,685	27,221	26,909	24,959	22,766	20,350	18,788	17,906	15,028
SOUTHEAST	19,338	20,762	20,293	19,695	15,292	13,833	13,475	12,575	10,699
EAST	66,697	66,679	66,942	63,417	62,502	59,355	49,721	46,177	37,702
NORTHEAST	9,758	10,584	10,023	9,044	8,177	7,384	6,678	6,443	5,433
MIDLANDS	12,697	14,208	13,419	12,750	10,779	9,144	9,039	8,257	6,965
STATE	171,596	182,523	179,306	166,767	151,821	137,657	125,722	118,995	99,216

1986 CONTINUED

COUNTIES	AGED 45-49	AGED 50-54	AGED 55-59	AGED 60-64	AGED 65-69	AGED 70-74	AGED 75-79	AGED 80+	ALL AGES	COUNTIES
DONEGAL	2,989	2,684	2,695	2,630	2,802	2,568	1,776	1,374	66,915	DONEGAL
LEITRIM	0,667	0,658	0,336	0,609	0,831	0,790	0,478	0,354	14,139	LEITRIM
SLIGO	1,322	1,259	1,336	1,203	1,251	0,754	0,547		28,808	SLIGO
GALWAY	4,367	3,831	3,585	3,467	3,547	3,192	2,814	2,187	91,179	GALWAY
MAYO	2,631	2,622	2,587	2,591	2,819	2,810	1,889	1,342	59,017	MAYO
CLARE	2,332	2,311	1,956	1,873	1,861	1,629	1,061	0,805	47,705	CLARE
LIMERICK – BOR	1,401	1,305	1,215	1,107	0,944	0,649	0,395	0,273	29,344	LIMERICK – BOR
LIMERICK – CO	2,623	2,345	2,131	2,011	1,986	1,570	1,010	0,631	54,605	LIMERICK – CO
TIPPERARY – NR	1,341	1,361	1,316	1,310	1,251	0,957	0,661	0,508	30,094	TIPPERARY – NR
CORK – BOR	3,260	3,091	2,934	2,453	1,831	0,951	0,634		64,907	CORK – BOR
CORK – CO	6,627	5,793	5,453	5,539	4,385	2,814	2,034	2,034	143,601	CORK – CO
KERRY	3,055	2,815	2,797	2,768	3,000	1,887	1,143	1,143	64,303	KERRY
CARLOW	0,982	0,850	0,859	0,791	0,641	0,507	0,335	0,240	20,800	CARLOW
KILKENNY	1,672	1,525	1,590	1,535	1,516	1,118	0,708	0,501	38,143	KILKENNY
TIPPERARY – SR	1,806	1,660	1,696	1,742	1,511	1,151	0,749	0,551	40,328	TIPPERARY – SR
WATERFORD – BOR	1,038	0,938	0,724	0,674	0,516	0,389	0,287	0,187	19,878	WATERFORD – BOR
WATERFORD – CO	1,238	1,125	1,081	1,084	1,026	0,813	0,522	0,356	26,138	WATERFORD – CO
WEXFORD	2,543	2,121	2,058	1,943	1,735	1,472	1,078	1,078	51,078	WEXFORD
DUBLIN – BOR	10,957	11,241	11,343	10,276	8,371	6,348	4,000	2,755	221,095	DUBLIN – BOR
DUN LAOIRE	1,217	1,186	1,155	1,048	0,854	0,748	0,526	0,375	24,095	DUN LAOIRE
DUBLIN – CO	11,834	8,770	6,641	5,100	4,031	2,833	1,628	1,085	258,774	DUBLIN – CO
KILDARE	2,561	2,030	1,752	1,605	1,439	1,013	0,678	0,437	61,680	KILDARE
WICKLOW	2,323	1,954	1,615	1,429	1,103	0,733	0,580	0,580	47,859	WICKLOW
MEATH	2,302	1,940	1,835	1,736	1,526	1,245	0,753	0,556	54,663	MEATH
CAVAN	1,229	1,288	1,405	1,336	1,312	1,141	0,716	0,503	27,865	CAVAN
LOUTH	2,164	1,811	1,607	1,715	1,457	1,104	0,664	0,475	46,051	LOUTH
MONAGHAN	1,139	1,155	1,172	1,166	1,100	0,910	0,601	0,420	27,418	MONAGHAN
LAOIS	1,201	1,090	1,119	1,191	0,849	0,637	0,517	0,380	27,838	LAOIS
LONGFORD	0,726	0,755	0,677	0,737	0,745	0,549	0,340	0,274	16,514	LONGFORD
OFFALY	1,369	1,312	1,270	1,281	1,203	0,867	0,586	0,436	30,930	OFFALY
ROSCOMMON	1,300	1,355	1,466	1,376	1,409	1,351	0,838	0,631	28,421	ROSCOMMON
WESTMEATH	1,459	1,360	1,339	1,358	1,110	0,857	0,509	0,467	32,484	WESTMEATH

REGIONS	AGED 45-49	AGED 50-54	AGED 55-59	AGED 60-64	AGED 65-69	AGED 70-74	AGED 75-79	AGED 80+	ALL AGES	REGIONS
DONEGAL	2,989	2,684	2,605	2,630	2,802	2,568	1,776	1,374	66,915	DONEGAL
NORTHWEST	1,989	1,917	2,072	2,001	2,091	1,903	1,232	0,896	42,947	NORTHWEST
WEST	7,058	6,453	6,172	6,135	6,011	6,011	4,076	3,022	150,196	WEST
MIDWEST	7,697	7,022	6,618	6,301	5,942	4,805	3,127	2,217	161,928	MIDWEST
SOUTHWEST	12,937	11,699	11,048	10,560	10,277	8,495	5,455	3,811	272,806	SOUTHWEST
SOUTHEAST	9,279	8,210	8,039	7,766	6,858	5,450	3,679	2,644	197,355	SOUTHEAST
EAST	31,274	27,121	24,318	21,264	17,590	13,290	8,318	5,789	668,164	EAST
NORTHEAST	4,532	4,254	4,184	4,217	3,889	3,155	1,981	1,398	101,334	NORTHEAST
MIDLANDS	6,055	5,880	5,891	5,946	5,559	4,561	2,879	2,167	136,196	MIDLANDS

| STATE | 83,810 | 75,249 | 71,006 | 66,643 | 61,452 | 50,328 | 32,523 | 23,317 | 1,797,911 | STATE |

102

COUNTIES	AGED 0-4	AGED 5-9	AGED 10-14	AGED 15-19	AGED 20-24	AGED 25-29	AGED 30-34	AGED 35-39	AGED 40-44
DONEGAL	6,187	7,170	6,720	5,824	4,464	3,614	3,931	3,983	3,202
LEITRIM	1,147	1,201	1,133	977	716	628	806	735	601
SLIGO	2,330	2,686	2,634	2,363	2,014	1,962	1,962	1,813	1,396
GALWAY	7,565	8,691	8,650	7,852	6,984	6,097	5,949	5,526	4,526
MAYO	5,139	5,722	5,560	4,895	3,508	2,673	3,541	3,367	2,687
CLARE	4,267	4,865	4,638	3,827	2,791	2,566	3,082	3,196	2,481
LIMERICK – BOR	2,844	2,488	2,753	3,005	3,276	2,554	1,834	1,666	1,471
LIMERICK – CO	4,786	5,577	5,432	4,423	3,593	3,443	3,832	3,629	3,025
TIPPERARY – NR	2,650	2,921	2,898	2,637	2,112	1,717	1,880	1,772	1,518
CORK – BOR	5,360	5,095	5,763	6,485	7,319	6,322	3,712	3,576	3,394
CORK – CO	12,990	14,657	5,964	15,580	9,023	8,643	10,177	9,575	7,745
KERRY	5,287	6,030	5,540	5,197	4,024	3,479	3,936	3,766	3,124
CARLOW	1,960	2,149	2,100	1,822	1,625	1,502	1,367	1,281	1,058
KILKENNY	3,484	3,898	3,550	3,278	2,534	2,416	2,589	2,285	1,952
TIPPERARY – SR	3,533	3,009	3,787	3,181	2,702	2,334	2,447	2,336	1,848
WATERFORD – BOR	1,699	1,938	1,977	2,027	1,935	1,680	1,237	1,242	1,131
WATERFORD – CO	2,202	2,662	2,497	2,182	1,763	1,472	1,741	1,560	1,374
WEXFORD	4,799	5,305	5,092	4,523	3,537	3,259	3,232	3,140	2,731
DUBLIN – BOR	15,037	11,722	16,998	22,861	31,274	27,462	12,253	11,713	11,403
DUN LAOIRE	2,136	2,628	1,907	2,482	3,063	2,521	1,460	1,430	1,502
DUBLIN – CO	28,747	31,886	27,956	22,790	10,826	21,554	25,019	21,474	16,052
KILDARE	6,355	6,389	6,192	4,825	4,170	4,600	5,024	4,607	3,426
WICKLOW	4,715	5,050	4,930	4,171	3,508	3,418	3,573	3,528	3,010
MEATH	5,546	6,146	5,569	4,588	3,623	3,502	4,030	3,723	2,493
CAVAN	2,332	2,642	2,442	2,151	1,583	1,374	1,617	1,508	1,181
LOUTH	4,302	4,663	4,557	4,287	3,808	3,610	3,054	2,984	2,493
MONAGHAN	2,471	2,796	2,411	2,198	1,730	1,649	1,683	1,607	1,242
LAOIS	2,551	2,827	2,585	2,218	1,827	1,636	1,750	1,508	1,297
LONGFORD	1,416	1,568	1,445	1,385	1,009	883	1,010	1,012	792
OFFALY	2,765	3,125	3,039	2,681	2,118	1,738	1,885	1,760	1,489
ROSCOMMON	2,426	2,747	2,547	2,141	1,509	1,182	1,540	1,489	1,277
WESTMEATH	2,071	3,247	3,322	2,900	2,372	2,069	2,197	1,988	1,625

REGIONS	AGED 0-4	AGED 5-9	AGED 10-14	AGED 15-19	AGED 20-24	AGED 25-29	AGED 30-34	AGED 35-39	AGED 40-44
DONEGAL	6,187	7,170	6,720	5,821	4,464	3,614	3,931	3,983	3,202
NORTHWEST	3,477	3,887	3,767	3,340	2,730	2,448	2,768	2,548	1,997
WEST	12,704	14,116	14,219	12,747	10,492	8,770	9,490	8,893	7,213
MIDWEST	14,547	15,871	15,721	13,892	11,772	10,280	10,628	10,263	7,495
SOUTHWEST	23,637	25,782	25,367	23,262	20,305	18,444	17,859	16,867	14,263
SOUTHEAST	17,886	19,852	19,207	17,026	14,116	12,663	12,613	11,853	10,094
EAST	62,506	63,021	63,542	61,717	65,403	63,066	61,354	46,475	38,280
NORTHEAST	9,215	10,101	9,410	8,636	7,121	6,633	6,354	6,099	4,916
MIDLANDS	12,159	13,514	12,938	11,325	8,665	7,508	8,382	7,766	6,480

STATE	AGED 0-4	AGED 5-9	AGED 10-14	AGED 15-19	AGED 20-24	AGED 25-29	AGED 30-34	AGED 35-39	AGED 40-44
STATE	162,318	173,614	170,691	157,769	145,478	133,426	123,375	114,747	94,940

FEMALES

1986 CONTINUED

COUNTIES	AGED 45-49	AGED 50-54	AGED 55-59	AGED 60-64	AGED 65-69	AGED 70-74	AGED 75-79	AGED 80+	ALL AGES
DONEGAL	2,744	2,320	2,467	2,626	2,758	2,630	1,903	1,851	64,394
LEITRIM	0,559	0,560	0,617	0,669	0,754	0,707	0,449	0,436	12,695
SLIGO	1,245	1,069	1,222	1,357	1,300	1,228	0,816	0,861	28,116
GALWAY	3,744	3,438	3,445	3,548	3,441	3,441	2,194	2,219	87,344
MAYO	2,356	2,221	2,391	2,668	2,982	2,864	1,859	1,807	56,240
CLARE	1,974	1,709	1,776	1,762	1,779	1,643	1,075	1,155	44,586
LIMERICK – BOR	1,385	1,342	1,308	1,244	1,328	1,009	0,737	0,618	30,662
LIMERICK – CO	2,316	2,005	1,960	1,976	1,809	1,738	1,189	1,122	52,185
TIPPERARY – NR	1,210	1,288	1,298	1,422	1,422	1,011	0,782	0,777	29,077
CORK – BOR	3,401	3,258	3,104	2,741	2,741	2,502	1,800	1,286	68,733
KERRY	2,640	2,420	2,503	2,732	2,825	2,775	1,863	1,622	60,200
CORK – CO	5,955	5,435	5,382	5,581	5,615	4,900	3,500	3,286	137,682
CARLOW	0,863	0,824	0,771	0,815	0,825	0,616	0,457	0,437	20,427
KILKENNY	1,564	1,456	1,448	1,500	1,474	1,199	0,839	0,801	36,190
TIPPERARY – SR	1,614	1,544	1,659	1,709	1,557	1,340	0,933	0,900	37,520
WATERFORD – BOR	1,032	0,909	0,810	0,790	0,661	0,612	0,494	0,455	20,824
WATERFORD – CO	0,664	1,071	0,985	1,092	1,044	0,900	0,585	0,605	24,799
WEXFORD	2,192	2,060	2,057	2,160	1,970	1,682	1,295	1,291	50,390
DUBLIN – BOR	12,203	12,739	13,429	13,199	11,767	10,430	7,723	7,777	250,170
DUN LAOIRE	1,509	1,464	1,454	1,426	1,467	1,290	0,777	1,160	29,025
DUBLIN – CO	11,811	8,663	6,996	5,892	5,118	3,961	2,724	1,603	263,072
KILDARE	2,379	1,873	1,663	1,656	1,573	1,255	0,858	0,714	57,404
WICKLOW	2,162	1,827	1,792	1,668	1,360	1,360	1,048	1,078	48,288
MEATH	2,171	1,893	1,748	1,717	1,636	1,335	1,072	0,867	52,013
CAVAN	1,043	1,114	1,135	1,292	1,311	1,431	0,872	0,685	25,228
LOUTH	2,011	1,764	1,795	1,977	1,782	1,135	0,961	0,936	46,505
MONAGHAN	1,089	1,041	1,039	1,079	1,026	0,930	0,684	0,654	25,437
LAOIS	1,063	1,045	1,075	1,054	0,971	0,840	0,603	0,587	25,336
LONGFORD	0,600	0,617	0,743	0,731	0,731	0,571	0,375	0,375	15,336
OFFALY	1,275	1,181	1,201	1,265	1,108	0,872	0,569	0,651	28,761
ROSCOMMON	1,117	1,174	1,318	1,309	1,343	1,256	0,791	0,831	25,097
WESTMEATH	1,380	1,278	1,318	1,359	1,132	0,968	0,664	0,693	31,497

REGIONS	AGED 45-49	AGED 50-54	AGED 55-59	AGED 60-64	AGED 65-69	AGED 70-74	AGED 75-79	AGED 80+	ALL AGES
DONEGAL	2,744	2,320	2,467	2,626	2,758	2,630	1,903	1,851	64,394
NORTHWEST	1,804	1,629	1,839	2,026	2,054	1,935	1,265	1,297	40,811
WEST	6,100	5,659	5,836	6,531	6,305	6,305	4,053	4,026	143,584
MIDWEST	6,885	6,344	6,342	6,547	6,072	5,401	3,783	3,667	156,510
SOUTHWEST	12,008	11,113	11,079	11,288	11,185	10,177	7,253	6,735	266,705
SOUTHEAST	8,329	7,864	7,730	8,075	7,075	6,349	4,603	4,581	190,150
EAST	32,235	28,465	27,082	25,558	23,051	19,662	14,342	14,208	700,062
NORTHEAST	4,143	3,919	3,969	4,348	4,119	3,496	2,328	2,275	97,082
MIDLANDS	5,435	5,295	5,628	5,730	5,285	4,579	3,002	3,137	127,028
STATE	79,683	72,608	71,972	72,329	68,533	60,534	42,532	41,777	1,786,326

104

PERSONS   1986 CONTINUED

COUNTIES	AGED 0-4	AGED 5-9	AGED 10-14	AGED 15-19	AGED 20-24	AGED 25-29	AGED 30-34	AGED 35-39	AGED 40-44
DONEGAL	12,553	14,511	13,577	11,079	9,159	7,418	8,111	8,201	6,983
LEITRIM	2,316	2,523	2,369	2,038	1,627	1,463	1,659	1,576	1,298
SLIGO	4,963	5,488	5,303	4,888	4,001	3,575	3,872	3,792	2,977
GALWAY	15,767	17,723	17,599	16,139	17,347	12,360	11,985	11,455	9,600
MAYO	10,281	11,734	10,402	10,909	9,313	5,871	7,259	7,200	5,911
CLARE	8,876	9,913	9,467	7,890	6,073	5,613	6,290	6,569	5,289
LIMERICK – BOR	5,635	5,045	5,687	6,101	6,295	5,291	3,734	3,364	2,894
LIMERICK – CO	9,646	11,436	11,059	9,317	7,702	7,279	7,930	7,497	6,282
TIPPERARY – NR	5,293	6,040	5,984	5,344	4,464	3,833	3,798	3,670	3,062
CORK – BOR	10,932	10,383	11,927	13,405	14,683	12,647	7,806	7,010	6,662
CORK – CO	26,534	30,113	28,247	24,162	19,827	18,650	20,602	19,819	15,909
KERRY	10,856	12,507	12,102	10,654	8,653	7,497	8,230	7,944	6,720
CARLOW	4,063	4,429	4,307	3,725	3,322	3,055	2,850	2,620	2,185
KILKENNY	7,299	7,022	7,383	6,540	5,411	5,193	5,187	4,842	4,078
TIPPERARY – SR	7,465	7,995	7,830	7,258	6,167	5,026	5,298	4,820	3,888
WATERFORD – BOR	3,903	3,937	3,979	4,140	3,761	3,146	2,550	2,446	2,249
WATERFORD – CO	4,573	5,535	5,684	4,580	3,833	3,201	3,521	3,292	2,790
WEXFORD	9,921	10,796	10,517	9,469	7,634	6,875	6,682	6,408	5,603
DUBLIN – BOR	31,332	24,264	34,706	45,205	50,423	53,100	24,378	22,386	21,908
DUN LAOIRE	4,295	3,341	3,914	4,826	5,591	4,722	2,941	2,735	2,750
DUBLIN – CO	59,232	65,756	57,142	46,435	43,527	41,037	48,500	43,141	32,010
KILDARE	13,137	13,446	13,033	10,602	9,179	9,468	10,143	9,496	7,217
WICKLOW	9,629	10,344	10,105	8,360	7,070	6,862	7,010	7,161	5,809
MEATH	11,528	12,547	11,584	9,697	7,205	7,732	8,010	7,733	6,289
CAVAN	4,733	5,328	5,012	4,466	3,685	3,307	3,414	3,209	2,591
LOUTH	9,141	9,504	9,308	8,680	7,723	7,158	6,297	5,975	5,107
MONAGHAN	5,099	5,853	5,113	4,525	3,800	3,552	3,521	3,358	2,651
LAOIS	5,339	5,812	5,288	4,887	4,113	3,637	3,628	3,147	2,740
LONGFORD	2,966	3,321	3,080	2,806	2,227	1,907	2,154	2,113	1,622
OFFALY	5,730	6,430	6,270	5,626	4,828	3,920	3,846	3,577	3,032
ROSCOMMON	4,816	5,502	5,180	4,658	3,361	2,836	3,312	3,001	2,707
WESTMEATH	6,003	6,567	6,539	6,098	5,115	4,352	4,481	4,105	3,344

REGIONS	AGED 0-4	AGED 5-9	AGED 10-14	AGED 15-19	AGED 20-24	AGED 25-29	AGED 30-34	AGED 35-39	AGED 40-44
DONEGAL	12,553	14,511	13,577	11,079	9,159	7,418	8,111	8,201	6,983
NORTHWEST	7,279	8,011	7,672	6,926	5,718	5,038	5,531	5,368	4,275
WEST	26,048	29,457	28,001	27,048	26,660	18,231	19,244	18,655	15,511
MIDWEST	29,456	32,434	32,197	28,652	24,534	22,016	21,752	21,100	17,527
SOUTHWEST	48,322	53,003	52,276	48,221	43,163	38,794	36,638	34,773	29,291
SOUTHEAST	37,224	40,614	39,100	35,721	30,128	26,496	26,088	24,428	20,793
EAST	129,203	129,700	130,484	125,134	122,995	122,421	101,080	92,652	75,982
NORTHEAST	18,973	20,685	19,433	17,680	15,298	14,017	13,232	12,542	10,349
MIDLANDS	24,856	27,722	26,357	24,075	19,644	16,652	17,471	16,023	13,445
STATE	333,914	356,137	349,097	324,536	297,299	271,083	249,097	233,742	194,156

105

PERSONS — 1986 CONTINUED

COUNTIES	AGED 45-49	AGED 50-54	AGED 55-59	AGED 60-64	AGED 65-69	AGED 70-74	AGED 75-79	AGED 80+	ALL AGES
DONEGAL	5,733	5,004	5,162	5,256	5,560	5,198	3,679	3,225	131,309
LEITRIM	1,226	1,218	1,353	1,367	1,587	1,497	927	790	26,834
SLIGO	2,567	2,328	2,558	2,560	2,431	2,558	1,570	1,403	56,924
GALWAY	8,111	7,269	7,030	6,930	6,633	5,995	4,381	3,890	178,527
MAYO	5,047	4,843	5,259	5,250	5,870	5,683	3,748	3,149	115,287
CLARE	4,306	3,720	3,635	3,640	3,277	3,748	2,116	1,960	92,381
LIMERICK – BOR	2,786	2,687	2,351	1,672	1,658	1,132	960	891	60,006
LIMERICK – CO	4,939	4,001	4,130	3,862	3,308	2,109	1,753	1,753	106,880
TIPPERARY – NR	2,551	2,649	2,732	2,440	1,968	1,443	1,280	1,280	59,171
CORK – BOR	6,664	6,349	5,902	5,425	5,454	2,944	2,461	2,461	133,725
CORK – CO	12,582	11,229	10,935	10,923	9,295	6,314	5,320	5,320	281,283
KERRY	5,600	5,235	5,300	5,837	5,454	3,550	2,765	2,765	124,593
CARLOW	1,845	1,674	1,606	1,414	1,123	792	677	677	74,317
KILKENNY	3,236	2,981	3,043	3,041	2,317	1,547	1,304	1,304	74,333
TIPPERARY – SR	3,420	3,038	3,451	3,068	2,491	1,682	1,541	1,541	77,884
WATERFORD – BOR	2,079	2,204	1,534	1,464	1,190	781	642	642	40,707
WATERFORD – CO	2,302	1,847	2,066	2,070	1,713	1,107	961	961	50,337
WEXFORD	4,735	4,115	4,100	3,705	3,154	2,373	2,100	2,368	102,368
DUBLIN – BOR	23,160	24,772	23,475	20,141	16,778	11,723	10,532	471,263	
DUN LAOIRE	7,726	7,650	7,474	2,321	2,036	1,643	1,544	92,556	
DUBLIN – CO	23,645	17,433	13,614	10,992	6,704	4,352	3,688	521,846	
KILDARE	4,940	3,303	3,261	2,029	2,268	1,536	1,151	110,174	
WICKLOW	4,485	3,781	3,407	3,167	2,463	1,781	1,658	94,147	
MEATH	4,553	3,839	3,453	3,162	2,611	1,625	1,423	106,676	
CAVAN	3,272	3,102	2,549	2,643	2,276	1,399	1,188	53,093	
LOUTH	4,175	3,575	3,602	3,239	2,535	1,625	1,411	92,556	
MONAGHAN	2,228	2,196	2,245	2,126	1,840	1,285	1,074	52,767	
LAOIS	2,264	2,135	2,214	2,043	1,689	1,120	976	53,275	
LONGFORD	1,326	1,372	1,379	1,476	1,739	715	624	31,850	
OFFALY	2,541	2,371	2,546	2,311	1,739	1,155	1,087	59,700	
ROSCOMMON	2,417	2,529	2,685	2,752	2,607	1,462	54,418		
WESTMEATH	2,810	2,646	2,717	2,262	1,925	1,262	1,155	63,981	

REGIONS									
DONEGAL	5,733	5,004	5,162	5,256	5,560	5,198	3,225	131,309	
NORTHWEST	3,793	3,546	3,911	3,927	4,145	2,497	2,193	83,758	
WEST	13,158	12,112	12,008	12,189	12,316	8,129	7,048	293,780	
MIDWEST	14,582	13,366	12,960	12,965	12,316	6,910	318,438		
SOUTHWEST	24,945	22,812	22,127	21,848	21,462	12,708	10,546	539,601	
SOUTHEAST	17,608	15,738	15,841	21,462	11,709	8,282	7,225	387,505	
EAST	63,500	55,586	46,822	44,337	32,962	22,660	19,996	1366,226	
NORTHEAST	8,675	8,173	8,153	8,565	6,651	4,309	3,673	198,416	
MIDLANDS	11,490	11,175	11,519	11,676	9,140	5,881	5,304	263,224	

| STATE | 163,493 | 147,857 | 142,978 | 138,972 | 129,985 | 110,862 | 75,055 | 65,094 | 3584,257 |

106

ESTIMATED POPULATION, 1991

MALES

COUNTIES	AGED 0-4	AGED 5-9	AGED 10-14	AGED 15-19	AGED 20-24	AGED 25-29	AGED 30-34	AGED 35-39	AGED 40-44
DONEGAL	5,160	6,878	7,603	6,477	5,150	4,357	3,968	4,360	4,323
LEITRIM	0,811	1,209	1,301	1,064	2,785	0,755	0,831	0,836	0,831
SLIGO	2,131	2,732	2,853	2,480	2,050	1,860	1,870	1,999	2,035
GALWAY	6,582	8,386	9,275	9,653	7,287	6,762	6,335	6,225	6,063
MAYO	3,850	5,523	6,068	5,116	3,465	3,237	3,302	3,901	3,952
CLARE	3,800	4,902	5,163	4,550	2,715	2,818	3,302	3,338	3,469
LIMERICK – BOR	2,465	2,407	2,350	2,350	2,711	2,818	2,535	1,704	1,504
LIMERICK – CO	4,032	5,268	5,672	5,350	4,288	4,067	4,128	4,310	3,993
TIPPERARY – NR	1,895	2,631	3,042	2,779	2,238	2,150	2,053	1,994	1,862
CORK – BOR	2,042	1,786	4,831	5,745	6,421	6,760	5,707	3,655	2,723
CORK – CO	11,118	14,291	15,730	13,766	11,107	10,707	10,719	10,807	10,336
KERRY	1,313	2,776	3,470	3,710	4,533	4,158	4,129	4,368	4,226
CARLOW	1,662	2,041	2,253	2,035	1,647	1,618	1,593	1,504	1,336
KILKENNY	3,036	4,038	4,056	3,554	2,886	2,809	2,850	2,754	2,508
TIPPERARY – SR	3,103	4,001	4,132	3,005	3,233	3,229	2,735	2,757	1,176
WATERFORD – BOR	1,342	1,804	2,013	1,777	1,318	1,860	1,149	1,263	1,176
WATERFORD – CO	1,361	2,105	2,844	2,353	2,024	1,903	1,770	1,772	1,706
WEXFORD	3,095	5,087	5,457	4,077	4,212	3,886	3,683	3,414	3,274
DUBLIN – BOR	12,275	9,552	9,310	15,805	21,957	24,471	19,201	8,476	8,766
DUN LAOIRE	1,856	1,782	1,564	1,895	2,146	2,364	1,892	1,300	1,230
DUBLIN – CO	31,336	35,173	36,072	22,063	23,161	23,167	24,044	26,686	22,686
KILDARE	6,338	7,150	7,152	6,641	5,462	5,535	5,452	5,512	5,066
WICKLOW	4,338	5,183	5,426	5,005	3,760	3,784	3,753	3,734	3,723
MEATH	5,127	6,572	6,602	5,800	3,583	4,280	4,115	4,297	4,185
CAVAN	1,674	2,335	2,649	2,311	1,852	1,906	1,907	1,770	1,655
LOUTH	4,614	4,614	4,766	4,430	3,003	3,874	3,156	3,217	2,940
MONAGHAN	2,214	2,774	3,052	2,522	2,025	2,052	1,809	1,850	1,736
LAOIS	2,113	2,441	3,004	2,526	2,208	2,226	1,805	1,882	1,632
LONGFORD	1,155	1,561	1,759	1,517	1,143	1,127	1,057	1,182	1,003
OFFALY	2,456	3,012	2,265	3,012	2,473	2,472	2,186	1,936	1,772
ROSCOMMON	1,743	2,653	2,895	2,335	1,963	1,564	1,654	1,922	1,605
WESTMEATH	2,370	3,052	3,382	3,076	2,634	2,579	2,384	2,348	2,153

REGIONS	AGED 0-4	AGED 5-9	AGED 10-14	AGED 15-19	AGED 20-24	AGED 25-29	AGED 30-34	AGED 35-39	AGED 40-44
DONEGAL	5,160	6,878	7,603	6,477	5,150	4,357	3,968	4,360	4,323
NORTHWEST	2,042	3,041	4,154	3,553	2,835	2,624	2,701	2,835	2,866
WEST	10,432	13,903	15,343	15,760	10,959	9,810	9,665	10,176	10,015
MIDWEST	12,291	15,009	16,534	15,412	12,722	12,291	12,018	11,246	10,919
SOUTHWEST	20,473	24,863	27,049	25,221	22,061	21,924	20,555	18,830	17,785
SOUTHEAST	15,806	19,560	20,755	18,801	15,926	15,314	14,089	13,464	12,566
EAST	61,051	65,411	66,516	64,318	60,169	63,850	59,387	49,510	45,656
NORTHEAST	7,948	9,783	10,467	10,272	7,776	7,832	7,261	6,837	6,331
MIDLANDS	10,237	13,225	14,295	12,469	10,561	9,968	9,286	9,170	8,255
STATE	146,250	172,618	182,716	160,292	148,150	147,969	138,930	126,378	118,716

MALES

1991 CONTINUED

COUNTIES	AGED 45-49	AGED 50-54	AGED 55-59	AGED 60-64	AGED 65-69	AGED 70-74	AGED 75-79	AGED 80+	ALL AGES
DONEGAL	3,787	2,982	2,604	2,541	2,516	2,303	1,812	1,487	68,308
LEITRIM	659	640	668	668	650	666	530	366	13,236
SLIGO	1,551	1,308	1,220	1,121	1,015	818	818	580	28,834
GALWAY	5,091	4,269	3,254	3,253	2,418	2,418	1,818	1,805	92,033
MAYO	3,200	2,648	2,423	2,452	2,452	2,418	1,970	1,490	57,570
CLARE	2,807	2,255	1,774	1,742	1,742	1,474	970	857	49,198
LIMERICK – BOR	1,339	1,134	1,070	1,070	620	620	411	282	28,539
LIMERICK – CO	3,203	2,530	2,045	2,070	1,525	1,474	970	726	56,372
TIPPERARY – NR	1,485	1,278	1,180	1,318	1,078	978	648	523	29,091
CORK – CO	8,073	6,406	5,208	5,208	4,152	3,264	2,725	1,686	147,811
KERRY	3,566	2,942	2,574	2,586	2,380	1,814	1,814	1,288	63,567
CORK – BOR	3,003	2,947	2,705	2,497	2,400	1,446	914	686	63,076
CARLOW	1,105	947	765	765	699	400	247	247	21,069
KILKENNY	2,071	1,633	1,443	1,388	1,114	1,144	725	530	39,129
TIPPERARY – SR	2,003	1,710	1,568	1,529	1,529	1,265	725	530	40,428
WATERFORD – BOR	1,123	1,019	674	604	604	410	265	211	20,803
WATERFORD – CO	1,366	1,195	988	965	965	798	525	373	25,305
WEXFORD	2,851	2,184	1,757	1,757	1,257	1,304	1,003	868	52,250
DUBLIN – BOR	9,336	9,049	9,001	8,817	6,138	6,138	4,037	1,925	190,199
DUN LAOIRE	1,190	1,153	1,044	1,044	926	669	499	420	73,038
DUBLIN – CO	16,221	11,837	8,188	8,733	4,733	3,264	1,963	1,301	256,196
KILDARE	3,807	2,530	1,588	1,430	1,109	1,109	671	504	68,082
WICKLOW	2,990	2,302	1,499	1,306	1,306	760	621	588	51,133
MEATH	3,320	2,588	1,666	1,576	1,576	1,202	810	588	59,118
CAVAN	1,348	1,193	1,270	1,195	1,195	766	588	509	26,655
LOUTH	2,567	2,070	1,701	1,542	1,105	1,042	728	521	46,583
MONAGHAN	1,371	1,072	1,057	1,042	1,042	858	617	435	27,663
LAOIS	1,393	1,148	1,036	1,079	1,079	818	414	404	28,305
LONGFORD	826	700	683	683	683	571	248	248	16,369
OFFALY	1,518	1,333	1,161	1,161	1,142	944	592	450	30,947
ROSCOMMON	1,403	1,273	1,343	1,343	1,255	1,140	912	655	27,698
WESTMEATH	1,707	1,304	1,231	1,194	1,194	867	586	466	32,806

REGIONS	AGED 45-49	AGED 50-54	AGED 55-59	AGED 60-64	AGED 65-69	AGED 70-74	AGED 75-79	AGED 80+	ALL AGES
DONEGAL	3,787	2,982	2,604	2,541	2,516	2,303	1,812	1,487	68,308
NORTHWEST	2,210	1,948	1,827	1,888	1,771	1,681	1,348	946	42,070
WEST	8,291	6,917	6,151	5,677	5,711	5,326	4,208	3,285	149,603
MIDWEST	8,921	7,466	6,605	5,978	5,710	4,597	3,198	2,383	163,200
SOUTHWEST	14,732	12,417	11,023	10,070	9,611	7,978	5,706	4,147	274,454
SOUTHEAST	10,522	8,997	7,777	7,320	6,532	5,350	3,593	2,803	199,584
EAST	36,864	30,125	25,450	21,898	19,327	13,039	8,775	6,359	697,766
NORTHEAST	5,286	4,352	3,966	3,806	3,769	3,479	2,111	1,465	101,301
MIDLANDS	6,847	5,877	5,539	5,389	5,353	4,340	3,082	2,232	136,125

STATE	AGED 45-49	AGED 50-54	AGED 55-59	AGED 60-64	AGED 65-69	AGED 70-74	AGED 75-79	AGED 80+	ALL AGES
STATE	97,460	81,081	70,942	64,567	60,300	48,093	33,833	25,107	1,832,411

FEMALES   1991 CONTINUED

COUNTIES	AGED 0-4	AGED 5-9	AGED 10-14	AGED 15-19	AGED 20-24	AGED 25-29	AGED 30-34	AGED 35-39	AGED 40-44
DONEGAL	1,927	6,801	7,403	6,268	4,784	4,120	3,743	4,102	4,075
LEITRIM	2,723	1,134	1,171	0,962	0,642	0,569	0,671	0,836	0,731
SLIGO	1,961	2,443	2,748	2,455	1,939	1,879	1,952	2,032	1,865
GALWAY	6,135	7,742	8,904	8,284	6,796	6,435	6,352	6,187	5,654
MAYO	3,648	5,474	5,824	4,944	3,516	2,675	2,843	3,716	3,283
CLARE	3,533	4,568	4,984	4,213	3,074	2,700	2,880	3,257	3,283
LIMERICK – BOR	2,315	2,507	2,222	2,658	2,670	2,282	2,266	1,624	1,534
LIMERICK – CO	2,853	2,560	2,702	2,695	2,753	2,282	1,806	4,080	3,750
TIPPERARY – NR	1,286	2,531	2,036	2,695	2,021	1,925	5,552	3,262	1,740
CORK – BOR	1,718	4,670	4,607	5,481	6,233	6,837	9,585	3,262	3,200
CORK – CO	10,523	13,578	14,884	12,540	23,092	9,105	3,629	10,699	9,767
KERRY	4,067	5,500	6,127	5,385	1,020	3,544	1,583	4,010	3,747
CARLOW	1,520	1,932	2,102	1,917	1,513	1,591	2,591	1,409	1,265
KILKENNY	2,043	3,676	3,941	3,234	2,558	2,439	2,383	2,674	2,333
TIPPERARY – SR	3,043	3,555	3,848	3,375	2,513	2,424	1,608	2,460	2,357
WATERFORD – BOR	1,836	1,914	1,266	1,960	1,941	1,890	1,525	1,191	1,253
WATERFORD – CO	1,775	2,239	2,639	2,253	1,700	1,707	3,340	1,772	1,556
WEXFORD	3,724	4,404	5,289	4,580	3,654	3,458	20,257	3,458	3,153
DUBLIN – BOR	11,324	8,683	9,112	16,561	22,087	27,199	2,188	8,695	10,021
DUN LAOIRE	1,755	1,780	1,491	2,025	2,438	2,808	26,784	1,323	1,394
DUBLIN – CO	20,660	33,310	34,087	28,092	23,092	25,154	5,311	27,301	22,462
KILDARE	5,655	6,634	6,612	5,584	4,575	4,704	3,994	5,407	4,820
WICKLOW	4,168	6,003	5,257	4,748	3,771	3,721	3,566	3,848	3,660
MEATH	4,263	6,075	6,395	5,280	4,021	3,828	1,682	4,345	3,869
CAVAN	1,551	2,330	2,554	2,007	1,514	3,830	1,746	1,625	1,481
LOUTH	3,754	4,281	4,604	4,281	1,760	1,658	0,982	3,008	2,942
MONAGHAN	2,091	2,634	2,793	2,178	1,770	1,730	1,778	1,708	1,607
LAOIS	2,132	2,702	2,784	2,300	1,046	0,903	1,297	1,800	1,501
LONGFORD	1,115	1,434	1,528	1,311	2,064	1,970	2,195	1,077	1,039
OFFALY	2,254	2,806	3,665	2,746	1,404	1,148		1,807	1,779
ROSCOMMON	1,362	2,623	2,781	2,217	2,372	2,717	1,297	1,606	1,529
WESTMEATH	2,173	3,058	3,340	3,038			2,195	2,266	2,033

REGIONS	AGED 0-4	AGED 5-9	AGED 10-14	AGED 15-19	AGED 20-24	AGED 25-29	AGED 30-34	AGED 35-39	AGED 40-44
DONEGAL	1,927	6,801	7,103	6,268	4,784	4,120	3,713	4,102	4,075
NORTHWEST	2,684	3,637	3,910	3,417	2,581	2,448	2,623	2,868	2,596
WEST	9,843	13,216	14,732	13,229	10,312	10,105	9,195	9,903	9,081
MIDWEST	11,503	14,626	15,914	14,564	11,518	11,209	10,727	10,849	10,307
SOUTHWEST	19,338	23,748	25,708	17,328	13,883	19,549	18,766	17,961	16,904
SOUTHEAST	14,641	18,120	19,785	17,328	13,883	13,509	13,030	12,817	11,917
EAST	57,425	61,393	62,954	62,509	60,884	67,504	67,304	50,919	46,726
NORTHEAST	7,389	9,245	9,951	8,556	7,136	6,786	6,692	6,341	6,030
MIDLANDS	9,556	12,700	13,558	11,612	8,656	7,968	8,018	8,656	7,881

| STATE | 137,596 | 163,483 | 173,024 | 160,987 | 139,743 | 142,198 | 135,098 | 124,416 | 115,017 |

109

FEMALES

1991 CONTINUED

COUNTIES	AGED 45-49	AGED 50-54	AGED 55-59	AGED 60-64	AGED 65-69	AGED 70-74	AGED 75-79	AGED 80+	ALL AGES
DONEGAL	3,223	2,717	2,280	2,406	2,568	2,449	2,077	1,983	65,926
LEITRIM	502	554	540	576	657	656	529	430	12,033
SLIGO	1,386	1,207	1,657	1,502	1,302	1,157	955	891	28,431
GALWAY	4,550	3,729	3,320	3,285	3,160	2,701	2,371	2,371	80,091
MAYO	2,666	2,312	2,141	2,274	2,671	2,630	2,224	1,913	54,906
CLARE	2,160	1,982	1,676	1,722	1,553	1,263	1,161	1,161	45,975
LIMERICK – BOR	1,415	1,321	1,258	1,215	1,172	962	769	699	29,659
LIMERICK – CO	3,053	2,301	1,948	1,864	2,010	1,696	1,325	1,208	54,030
TIPPERARY – NR	1,186	1,170	1,251	1,253	1,331	1,021	794	818	28,503
CORK – BOR	3,215	3,313	3,103	2,873	2,816	2,378	1,977	1,960	66,306
CORK – CO	7,751	5,823	5,301	5,137	4,821	4,823	3,749	3,556	142,074
KERRY	3,001	2,587	2,372	2,457	2,652	2,499	2,131	1,804	59,717
CARLOW	1,074	831	802	730	797	656	486	461	20,668
KILKENNY	1,951	1,547	1,415	1,401	1,412	1,280	905	841	37,314
TIPPERARY – SR	1,811	1,500	1,482	1,560	1,616	1,311	1,023	1,007	37,258
WATERFORD – BOR	1,112	1,027	898	777	758	587	493	516	21,727
WATERFORD – CO	1,358	1,036	1,031	920	951	887	661	506	24,706
WEXFORD	2,703	2,195	1,853	1,978	2,060	1,700	1,300	1,366	50,653
DUBLIN – BOR	10,306	11,312	11,853	12,247	12,218	9,861	7,956	8,165	218,657
DUN LAOIRE	1,470	1,476	1,392	1,406	1,368	1,299	1,027	1,253	27,893
DUBLIN – CO	16,471	12,007	8,699	6,339	5,994	4,712	3,339	3,059	311,152
KILDARE	3,463	2,391	1,809	1,573	1,599	1,318	1,104	844	63,649
WICKLOW	3,045	2,182	1,805	1,711	1,610	1,417	1,104	1,190	51,830
MEATH	3,013	2,161	1,868	1,655	1,601	1,412	1,053	914	56,466
CAVAN	1,156	1,300	1,077	1,061	1,107	849	675	675	24,077
LOUTH	2,166	2,057	1,739	1,731	1,899	1,558	1,301	1,020	47,649
MONAGHAN	1,235	1,059	983	1,076	887	887	706	682	25,662
LAOIS	1,267	1,043	998	1,030	937	847	648	616	25,908
LONGFORD	770	586	600	685	719	627	379	379	15,350
OFFALY	1,471	1,233	1,158	1,128	1,189	947	670	644	28,829
ROSCOMMON	1,244	988	1,150	1,236	1,265	1,168	940	833	25,461
WESTMEATH	1,618	1,162	1,252	1,212	1,300	1,079	755	682	31,907

REGIONS	AGED 45-49	AGED 50-54	AGED 55-59	AGED 60-64	AGED 65-69	AGED 70-74	AGED 75-79	AGED 80+	ALL AGES
DONEGAL	3,223	2,717	2,280	2,406	2,568	2,449	2,077	1,983	65,926
NORTHWEST	1,978	1,761	1,597	1,778	1,950	1,813	1,484	1,321	40,464
WEST	7,216	6,941	5,470	5,559	6,003	4,929	4,284	3,886	143,907
MIDWEST	6,319	6,783	6,126	6,808	6,255	5,232	4,151	3,886	158,167
SOUTHWEST	14,052	11,723	10,776	10,464	10,879	7,897	7,329	7,329	268,167
SOUTHEAST	10,042	9,226	7,648	7,375	7,714	6,421	4,787	4,787	192,326
EAST	37,698	31,532	25,531	25,531	20,019	15,447	15,425	15,425	729,656
NORTHEAST	4,857	4,016	3,799	3,768	4,379	3,552	2,656	2,377	97,383
MIDLANDS	6,370	5,312	5,158	5,321	5,460	3,502	3,502	3,154	127,450

| STATE | 93,855 | 78,111 | 70,274 | 68,210 | 69,489 | 59,594 | 47,020 | 44,546 | 1,823,561 |

PERSONS

1991 CONTINUED

COUNTIES	AGED 0-4	AGED 5-9	AGED 10-14	AGED 15-19	AGED 20-24	AGED 25-29	AGED 30-34	AGED 35-39	AGED 40-44
DONEGAL	10,087	13,679	15,006	12,745	9,034	8,477	7,711	8,462	8,398
LEITRIM	1,534	2,403	2,472	2,026	1,427	1,324	1,502	1,672	1,562
SLIGO	3,032	5,175	5,601	4,744	3,082	3,748	3,822	4,031	3,900
GALWAY	12,777	16,128	18,179	16,037	14,093	13,102	12,687	12,412	11,717
MAYO	7,408	10,937	11,896	10,060	7,198	5,732	6,173	7,617	7,379
CLARE	7,312	9,471	10,147	8,772	6,550	5,937	6,182	6,595	6,752
LIMERICK – BOR	4,790	4,914	4,642	5,373	5,391	5,900	4,801	3,328	3,129
LIMERICK – CO	7,891	10,028	11,681	10,447	8,011	7,660	7,934	8,390	7,744
TIPPERARY – NR	3,781	5,222	5,078	5,384	4,259	4,094	3,828	3,782	3,602
CORK – BOR	9,200	9,456	9,528	11,226	12,654	13,806	11,259	6,596	6,513
CORK – CO	21,641	27,850	30,623	26,315	20,707	19,965	20,304	21,496	20,103
KERRY	7,380	11,296	12,696	11,095	8,553	7,702	7,758	8,379	8,073
CARLOW	3,182	3,976	4,355	3,052	3,160	3,209	3,176	2,813	2,601
KILKENNY	6,046	7,556	7,907	6,788	5,480	5,248	5,450	5,428	4,899
TIPPERARY – SR	3,785	7,711	7,980	7,280	5,752	5,653	5,118	5,217	4,465
WATERFORD – BOR	3,785	3,998	3,483	3,037	3,820	3,758	3,057	2,454	2,429
WATERFORD – CO	3,544	4,644	5,193	4,606	3,724	3,610	3,295	3,544	3,262
WEXFORD	7,719	9,891	10,746	8,566	7,366	7,344	7,023	6,725	6,427
DUBLIN – BOR	23,579	18,235	18,422	32,366	44,044	51,670	39,458	17,171	18,787
DUN LAOIRE	3,611	3,562	3,055	3,020	4,584	5,177	4,980	2,632	2,624
DUBLIN – CO	61,096	68,503	70,159	57,155	46,253	48,561	51,728	53,483	45,149
KILDARE	11,674	13,793	14,064	12,725	10,032	10,329	10,763	10,919	9,986
WICKLOW	9,506	10,091	10,693	9,651	7,531	7,505	7,533	7,582	7,383
MEATH	9,200	12,647	13,987	11,098	8,694	8,117	8,129	8,642	8,054
CAVAN	3,245	4,725	5,203	4,408	3,366	3,204	3,351	3,305	3,136
LOUTH	5,704	8,835	9,370	8,700	7,511	7,704	7,822	6,225	5,882
MONAGHAN	4,298	5,400	5,788	4,700	3,785	3,710	3,590	3,558	3,343
LAOIS	4,445	5,650	5,845	4,822	3,068	3,056	3,751	3,687	3,133
LONGFORD	2,270	2,095	3,317	2,828	2,189	2,030	2,039	2,254	2,132
OFFALY	4,713	5,818	5,330	5,758	4,537	4,442	3,984	3,843	3,551
ROSCOMMON	4,005	5,352	5,666	1,552	3,367	2,712	2,951	3,134	3,551
WESTMEATH	4,563	6,117	6,722	6,111	5,056	4,796	4,579	4,614	4,186

REGIONS									
DONEGAL	10,087	13,679	15,006	12,745	9,034	8,477	7,711	8,462	8,398
NORTHWEST	5,626	7,578	8,073	6,970	5,116	5,072	5,324	5,703	5,462
WEST	20,275	27,125	30,075	26,997	24,271	23,490	18,860	20,029	19,096
MIDWEST	23,774	29,635	32,448	29,976	24,240	23,490	22,745	22,095	21,226
SOUTHWEST	37,811	48,611	52,757	48,636	41,294	41,473	39,121	36,791	34,689
SOUTHEAST	30,647	37,660	40,540	36,129	27,815	28,823	27,119	26,281	24,483
EAST	118,476	126,831	129,170	126,717	121,053	131,354	121,691	100,429	91,887
NORTHEAST	15,337	19,028	20,418	17,828	14,962	14,618	13,953	13,178	12,361
MIDLANDS	19,793	25,925	27,853	24,081	19,217	17,936	17,304	17,826	16,136

| STATE | 293,846 | 336,101 | 356,640 | 330,279 | 287,002 | 290,167 | 274,028 | 250,794 | 233,733 |

111

PERSONS 1991 CONTINUED

COUNTIES	AGED 45-49	AGED 50-54	AGED 55-59	AGED 60-64	AGED 65-69	AGED 70-74	AGED 75-79	AGED 80+	ALL AGES
DONEGAL	7.010	5.693	4.884	4.947	5.094	4.752	3.880	3.470	134.234
LEITRIM	1.251	1.194	1.174	1.244	1.307	1.322	1.050	0.796	25.269
SLIGO	2.937	2.515	2.250	2.422	2.423	2.172	1.773	1.471	57.265
GALWAY	9.641	7.298	6.979	6.539	6.631	6.068	4.730	4.231	181.124
MAYO	5.866	4.950	4.697	4.607	5.123	5.048	3.393	3.393	112.476
CLARE	5.267	4.237	3.579	3.450	3.164	3.027	2.307	2.091	95.171
LIMERICK – BOR	2.754	2.655	2.572	2.285	1.582	1.587	1.180	1.091	58.198
LIMERICK – CO	6.348	4.900	4.169	3.848	3.221	2.349	1.934	1.802	110.402
TIPPERARY – NR	2.071	2.157	1.809	2.442	1.999	1.442	1.341	1.103	57.504
CORK – BOR	6.303	6.182	5.953	5.367	3.824	2.891	2.655	2.341	129.885
CORK – CO	15.821	12.229	10.769	10.145	9.025	6.767	5.729	5.779	289.885
KERRY	6.657	5.523	5.077	5.031	4.879	3.945	3.092	3.092	123.279
CARLOW	2.179	1.778	1.610	1.504	1.346	0.812	0.768	0.768	41.737
KILKENNY	4.325	3.180	2.873	2.844	2.294	1.630	1.380	1.380	76.443
TIPPERARY – SR	3.814	3.109	3.102	2.830	2.455	2.101	1.577	1.577	77.686
WATERFORD – BOR	2.265	1.787	1.451	1.451	1.145	0.758	0.727	0.727	42.530
WATERFORD – CO	2.724	2.231	2.088	2.016	1.997	0.960	0.611	0.611	50.611
WEXFORD	5.557	4.670	4.017	3.886	3.817	2.312	2.234	2.234	102.903
DUBLIN – BOR	19.642	21.252	22.042	20.935	15.900	11.993	11.090	11.090	408.856
DUN LAOIRE	7.661	8.634	8.485	8.450	2.224	1.526	1.673	1.673	50.841
DUBLIN – CO	32.691	23.844	17.190	13.127	10.767	5.307	4.360	4.360	617.348
KILDARE	7.270	4.321	3.744	3.161	2.776	1.630	1.348	1.348	131.731
WICKLOW	5.935	4.484	3.672	3.028	2.427	1.864	1.811	1.811	102.972
MEATH	6.363	4.519	3.737	3.210	2.514	1.893	1.502	1.502	115.584
CAVAN	2.504	2.194	2.270	2.340	2.149	1.615	1.234	1.234	50.777
LOUTH	5.033	4.027	3.440	3.201	2.607	1.829	1.541	1.541	94.637
MONAGHAN	2.606	2.147	2.055	2.033	1.745	1.323	1.117	1.117	53.375
LAOIS	2.660	2.191	2.017	2.066	1.665	1.226	1.020	1.020	54.213
LONGFORD	1.596	1.286	1.315	1.303	1.402	0.903	0.677	0.677	31.719
OFFALY	2.989	2.566	2.372	2.289	2.331	1.262	1.033	1.033	59.776
ROSCOMMON	2.617	2.361	2.437	2.570	2.520	1.952	1.488	1.488	53.150
WESTMEATH	3.325	2.785	2.556	2.473	2.494	1.841	1.148	1.148	64.708

REGIONS	AGED 45-49	AGED 50-54	AGED 55-59	AGED 60-64	AGED 65-69	AGED 70-74	AGED 75-79	AGED 80+	ALL AGES
DONEGAL	7.010	5.693	4.884	4.947	5.094	4.752	3.880	3.470	134.234
NORTHWEST	4.188	3.709	3.424	3.666	3.730	3.494	2.832	2.267	82.534
WEST	15.507	12.258	11.621	11.236	11.804	11.116	9.137	7.560	293.600
MIDWEST	17.340	14.249	12.731	11.986	11.965	9.829	7.340	6.269	321.367
SOUTHEAST	28.784	24.140	21.799	20.543	20.490	17.728	13.603	11.476	542.646
SOUTHWEST	20.564	17.223	15.425	14.695	14.646	11.771	8.470	7.590	391.910
EAST	74.562	61.657	52.870	47.420	43.306	33.498	24.222	21.784	1427.422
NORTHEAST	10.143	8.368	7.765	7.574	7.951	6.591	4.767	3.842	198.684
MIDLANDS	13.217	11.189	10.697	10.710	10.813	8.908	6.584	5.386	263.575
STATE	**191.315**	**159.192**	**141.216**	**132.777**	**129.789**	**107.687**	**80.853**	**69.653**	**3655.972**

112

ESTIMATED POPULATION, 1996

MALES

COUNTIES	AGED 0-4	AGED 5-9	AGED 10-14	AGED 15-19	AGED 20-24	AGED 25-29	AGED 30-34	AGED 35-39	AGED 40-44
DONEGAL	4,945	5,641	7,140	7,126	5,303	4,763	4,522	4,143	4,462
LEITRIM	1,677	2,053	1,188	1,116	0,766	0,627	0,749	0,826	0,826
SLIGO	1,968	2,237	2,783	2,642	1,067	1,828	1,993	1,957	2,054
GALWAY	6,218	6,780	8,632	8,003	7,256	6,634	6,811	6,518	6,355
MAYO	3,306	4,242	5,580	5,330	5,746	5,000	3,185	3,508	4,018
CLARE	3,583	4,117	5,019	4,837	3,732	3,400	3,491	3,429	3,432
LIMERICK – BOR	2,226	2,272	2,200	2,146	2,317	2,499	2,613	2,330	1,599
LIMERICK – CO	3,808	1,255	5,208	5,648	1,550	4,210	4,357	4,336	4,133
TIPPERARY – NR	1,707	1,882	2,554	1,457	2,215	2,031	2,004	2,027	1,857
CORK – BOR	1,637	1,261	4,330	1,457	2,256	6,037	6,340	5,301	3,302
CORK – CO	10,452	11,302	14,565	14,721	11,876	11,011	11,506	11,086	10,893
KERRY	3,272	4,553	5,778	5,285	4,730	4,031	4,266	4,199	4,414
CARLOW	1,541	1,618	2,009	2,061	1,730	1,559	1,657	1,612	1,500
KILKENNY	2,725	3,472	4,071	3,744	2,087	2,707	2,889	2,902	2,761
TIPPERARY – SR	2,796	3,182	4,046	3,950	3,002	2,986	2,874	2,740	2,770
WATERFORD – BOR	1,805	1,945	2,009	1,068	1,757	1,975	1,854	1,308	1,234
WATERFORD – CO	1,701	1,901	2,376	2,575	1,027	1,913	1,944	1,760	1,745
WEXFORD	3,692	3,973	5,053	4,967	4,142	4,016	3,952	3,644	3,427
DUBLIN – BOR	9,760	5,538	6,519	7,806	14,723	17,426	18,000	15,567	6,570
DUN LAOIRE	1,730	1,486	1,633	1,465	1,707	1,976	2,055	1,710	1,233
DUBLIN – CO	32,424	36,305	37,402	35,303	27,377	27,197	28,880	27,624	27,178
KILDARE	5,668	6,372	7,556	7,363	6,267	6,049	6,129	5,841	5,686
WICKLOW	4,206	4,625	5,315	5,102	4,288	3,949	4,092	3,950	3,822
MEATH	4,394	5,738	6,862	6,400	5,085	4,617	4,705	4,459	4,469
CAVAN	1,446	1,692	2,357	2,366	1,801	1,650	1,878	1,979	1,723
LOUTH	3,830	3,920	4,530	4,419	3,741	3,830	3,781	3,427	3,163
MONAGHAN	2,035	2,388	2,760	2,830	2,117	1,906	2,046	1,907	1,834
LAOIS	2,153	2,176	2,361	2,701	2,122	2,046	2,230	2,009	1,870
LONGFORD	1,151	1,198	1,567	1,622	1,196	1,046	1,150	1,093	1,173
OFFALY	2,273	2,512	2,973	3,020	2,469	2,252	2,475	2,160	1,903
ROSCOMMON	1,723	2,220	2,700	2,553	1,753	1,567	1,567	1,702	1,823
WESTMEATH	2,199	2,196	3,115	3,206	2,511	2,502	2,680	2,446	2,383

REGIONS

REGIONS	AGED 0-4	AGED 5-9	AGED 10-14	AGED 15-19	AGED 20-24	AGED 25-29	AGED 30-34	AGED 35-39	AGED 40-44
DONEGAL	4,945	5,641	7,140	7,126	5,303	4,763	4,522	4,143	4,462
NORTHWEST	2,615	3,000	3,371	3,758	2,733	2,455	2,732	2,770	2,880
WEST	9,611	11,031	14,212	14,283	11,002	9,534	10,016	12,026	10,373
MIDWEST	11,324	12,346	14,981	15,347	12,984	12,539	12,555	12,131	11,321
SOUTHWEST	19,031	20,726	24,693	25,158	21,776	21,074	22,121	20,586	18,699
SOUTHEAST	14,640	16,035	19,566	19,274	15,635	15,146	15,570	14,065	13,446
EAST	57,082	60,052	65,287	63,433	59,647	61,141	63,861	59,160	54,958
NORTHEAST	7,311	8,000	9,667	9,615	7,789	7,386	7,705	7,213	6,720
MIDLANDS	9,404	10,802	13,316	13,192	10,051	9,679	10,106	9,410	9,161
STATE	137,996	147,843	172,833	171,186	116,020	143,327	149,188	139,504	126,020

113

MALES

1996 CONTINUED

COUNTIES	ALL AGES	AGED 80+	AGED 75-79	AGED 70-74	AGED 65-69	AGED 60-64	AGED 55-59	AGED 50-54	AGED 45-49
DONEGAL	69.220	1.544	1.634	2.084	2.447	2.458	2.885	3.754	4.319
LEITRIM	12.226	0.397	0.417	0.524	0.627	0.576	0.617	0.633	0.700
SLIGO	28.644	0.627	0.691	0.909	1.113	1.090	1.239	1.522	1.997
GALWAY	92.222	1.869	2.038	2.689	3.060	3.313	4.063	4.060	6.063
MAYO	55.556	1.574	1.709	2.081	2.311	2.345	2.525	3.141	3.915
CLARE	50.152	0.897	1.012	1.384	1.660	1.735	2.113	2.715	3.157
LIMERICK – BOR	27.470	0.293	0.392	0.720	0.942	1.062	1.242	1.271	1.507
LIMERICK – CO	57.511	0.764	0.993	1.307	1.767	2.027	2.460	3.244	3.514
TIPPERARY – NR	27.826	0.521	0.662	0.925	1.076	1.135	1.179	1.418	1.787
CORK – BOR	60.809	0.692	0.924	1.596	2.124	2.545	2.829	2.007	3.043
CORK – CO	150.640	2.307	2.821	3.823	4.607	5.022	6.046	7.605	10.207
KERRY	62.216	1.104	1.613	2.055	2.423	2.491	2.825	3.541	4.135
CARLOW	21.037	0.244	0.314	0.528	0.660	0.719	0.900	1.066	1.310
KILKENNY	39.735	0.561	0.722	1.087	1.311	1.323	1.560	2.019	2.504
TIPPERARY – SR	40.107	0.569	0.744	1.160	1.356	1.426	1.624	2.312	2.463
WATERFORD – BOR	21.583	0.208	0.280	0.478	0.607	0.924	0.966	1.101	1.132
WATERFORD – CO	25.430	0.380	0.514	0.752	0.893	0.966	1.123	1.310	1.551
WEXFORD	52.042	0.848	0.950	1.414	1.738	1.853	2.339	2.885	3.249
DUBLIN – BOR	157.943	3.001	3.896	6.500	8.526	8.855	9.942	8.372	7.623
DUN LAOIRE	21.887	0.421	0.446	0.727	0.787	0.988	1.067	1.133	1.173
DUBLIN – CO	351.344	1.555	2.258	3.853	5.787	7.000	11.392	16.080	22.229
KILDARE	73.784	0.523	0.735	1.112	1.432	1.755	2.497	3.735	5.059
WICKLOW	53.912	0.649	0.756	1.116	1.404	1.723	2.199	3.266	3.777
MEATH	63.015	0.645	0.811	1.244	1.520	1.697	2.263	3.048	4.210
CAVAN	25.188	0.538	0.690	0.929	1.127	1.086	1.105	1.303	1.539
LOUTH	47.457	0.571	0.752	1.209	1.548	1.556	1.946	2.452	2.397
MONAGHAN	27.634	0.440	0.582	0.814	0.940	0.966	1.009	1.312	1.632
LAOIS	28.524	0.442	0.557	0.825	0.740	0.927	1.073	1.334	1.579
LONGFORD	16.061	0.287	0.370	0.524	0.538	0.652	0.663	0.737	1.035
OFFALY	30.651	0.469	0.644	0.898	1.038	1.110	1.234	1.478	1.743
ROSCOMMON	26.755	0.702	0.770	1.021	1.231	1.184	1.219	1.372	1.575
WESTMEATH	32.847	0.461	0.593	0.920	1.084	1.199	1.356	1.663	2.133

REGIONS	ALL AGES	AGED 80+	AGED 75-79	AGED 70-74	AGED 65-69	AGED 60-64	AGED 55-59	AGED 50-54	AGED 45-49
DONEGAL	69.220	1.544	1.634	2.084	2.447	2.458	2.885	3.754	4.319
NORTHWEST	40.870	1.024	1.138	1.433	1.770	1.666	1.856	2.162	2.787
WEST	147.778	3.443	3.747	4.770	5.303	5.658	6.588	8.110	9.373
MIDWEST	162.959	3.475	3.059	4.426	5.115	5.966	7.024	8.651	10.775
SOUTHWEST	273.665	4.303	5.358	7.474	9.724	10.059	11.700	14.153	17.441
SOUTHEAST	199.934	2.810	3.524	5.419	6.567	7.111	8.512	10.200	12.357
EAST	721.885	6.704	8.902	14.552	19.564	22.918	28.281	35.534	41.676
NORTHEAST	100.279	1.558	2.033	2.952	3.414	3.608	4.060	5.080	6.168
MIDLANDS	134.838	2.361	2.934	4.188	4.871	5.068	5.536	6.644	8.115

STATE	ALL AGES	AGED 80+	AGED 75-79	AGED 70-74	AGED 65-69	AGED 60-64	AGED 55-59	AGED 50-54	AGED 45-49
STATE	1851.428	26.402	32.329	47.298	58.725	64.511	76.442	94.288	116.616

114

COUNTIES	AGED 0-4	AGED 5-9	AGED 10-14	AGED 15-19	AGED 20-24	AGED 25-29	AGED 30-34	AGED 35-39	AGED 40-44	COUNTIES
DONEGAL	4,719	5,559	7,035	6,856	5,045	4,394	4,252	3,909	4,191	DONEGAL
LEITRIM	0,607	0,779	1,165	0,999	0,609	0,492	0,612	0,719	0,833	LEITRIM
SLIGO	1,811	2,082	2,504	2,542	1,969	1,709	2,009	2,020	2,082	SLIGO
GALWAY	6,850	6,305	7,052	8,117	7,205	6,191	6,683	6,597	6,113	GALWAY
MAYO	3,224	3,992	5,581	5,152	3,456	2,654	2,843	3,009	3,774	MAYO
CLARE	3,311	3,848	4,687	4,502	3,328	2,952	3,013	3,050	3,341	CLARE
LIMERICK – BOR	2,086	1,987	2,312	2,205	2,376	2,369	2,697	2,058	1,491	LIMERICK – BOR
LIMERICK – CO	3,642	4,047	5,065	5,273	4,235	3,729	3,964	4,019	4,199	LIMERICK – CO
TIPPERARY – NR	1,709	1,832	2,660	2,617	1,938	1,820	1,985	1,706	1,855	TIPPERARY – NR
CORK – BOR	3,112	4,076	4,272	4,440	5,228	5,698	6,067	5,082	3,022	CORK – BOR
CORK – CO	9,807	11,149	13,806	13,609	10,274	9,733	10,107	10,086	10,877	CORK – CO
KERRY	3,661	3,292	5,509	5,492	1,274	3,508	3,692	3,697	4,089	KERRY
CARLOW	1,410	1,683	1,804	1,903	1,551	1,470	1,571	1,692	1,397	CARLOW
KILKENNY	2,438	3,249	3,719	3,564	2,577	2,481	2,612	2,674	2,720	KILKENNY
TIPPERARY – SR	2,616	2,776	3,494	3,401	2,528	2,219	2,472	2,392	2,480	TIPPERARY – SR
WATERFORD – BOR	1,776	1,860	1,042	1,440	1,715	1,851	1,810	1,564	1,201	WATERFORD – BOR
WATERFORD – CO	1,616	1,819	2,216	2,367	1,715	1,631	1,762	1,557	1,767	WATERFORD – CO
WEXFORD	3,438	3,741	4,789	4,734	3,611	3,494	3,538	3,417	3,314	WEXFORD
DUBLIN – BOR	3,042	5,033	5,870	6,063	17,058	18,895	10,066	16,746	6,990	DUBLIN – BOR
DUN LAOIRE	1,635	1,405	1,643	1,621	1,990	2,177	2,475	2,054	1,287	DUN LAOIRE
DUBLIN – CO	30,576	34,386	35,520	33,616	27,107	28,162	30,406	29,052	28,284	DUBLIN – CO
KILDARE	5,516	5,058	6,859	6,239	5,189	5,144	5,493	5,493	5,618	KILDARE
WICKLOW	3,510	4,372	5,116	5,017	3,182	3,748	4,083	4,053	3,978	WICKLOW
MEATH	4,742	5,414	6,325	6,020	1,531	4,185	4,312	4,204	4,490	MEATH
CAVAN	1,321	1,552	2,241	2,183	1,472	1,210	1,449	1,449	1,598	CAVAN
LOUTH	3,554	3,653	4,222	4,290	3,816	3,901	3,786	3,521	2,964	LOUTH
MONAGHAN	1,909	2,235	2,631	2,517	1,606	1,674	1,689	1,795	1,707	MONAGHAN
LAOIS	1,018	2,299	2,666	2,467	1,705	1,660	1,839	1,795	1,793	LAOIS
LONGFORD	1,004	1,107	1,453	1,434	0,953	0,931	1,002	1,706	1,103	LONGFORD
OFFALY	2,024	2,303	2,746	2,747	2,064	1,871	2,031	1,817	1,916	OFFALY
ROSCOMMON	1,652	2,135	2,727	2,417	1,475	1,034	1,261	1,359	1,645	ROSCOMMON
WESTMEATH	2,030	2,286	3,152	3,030	2,430	2,198	2,313	2,261	2,311	WESTMEATH

REGIONS	AGED 0-4	AGED 5-9	AGED 10-14	AGED 15-19	AGED 20-24	AGED 25-29	AGED 30-34	AGED 35-39	AGED 40-44	REGIONS
DONEGAL	4,719	5,559	7,035	6,856	5,045	4,394	4,252	3,909	4,191	DONEGAL
NORTHWEST	2,418	2,852	3,669	3,531	2,576	2,282	2,621	2,719	2,915	NORTHWEST
WEST	10,283	10,387	13,533	13,599	10,461	8,845	9,526	9,596	10,087	WEST
MIDWEST	10,748	11,714	14,670	14,623	11,807	10,870	11,657	10,237	10,886	MIDWEST
SOUTHWEST	17,270	15,132	23,676	23,541	19,576	18,939	19,866	18,865	17,988	SOUTHWEST
SOUTHEAST	13,724	15,132	18,054	17,012	13,773	13,146	13,874	13,224	12,874	SOUTHEAST
EAST	55,535	56,575	61,333	61,567	60,337	62,511	66,735	61,860	50,647	EAST
NORTHEAST	6,703	7,445	9,094	8,090	6,934	6,794	6,840	6,676	6,269	NORTHEAST
MIDLANDS	8,775	10,129	12,744	12,095	8,667	7,694	8,476	8,280	8,768	MIDLANDS
STATE	129,755	139,312	163,808	162,714	139,208	135,475	143,847	136,096	124,625	STATE

COUNTIES	AGED 45-49	AGED 50-54	AGED 55-59	AGED 60-64	AGED 65-69	AGED 70-74	AGED 75-79	AGED 80+	ALL AGES	COUNTIES
DONEGAL	1,846	3,186	2,665	2,229	2,363	2,292	1,947	2,175	66,909	DONEGAL
LEITRIM	1,250	1,586	0,534	0,503	0,570	0,573	0,492	0,485	11,240	LEITRIM
SLIGO	2,061	1,346	1,190	1,046	1,150	1,163	0,905	1,005	28,474	SLIGO
GALWAY	5,665	4,519	3,611	3,175	3,268	3,062	2,496	2,793	90,021	GALWAY
MAYO	3,308	2,615	2,229	2,037	2,304	2,369	2,057	2,221	52,914	MAYO
CLARE	3,253	2,452	1,930	1,572	1,618	1,509	1,200	1,300	46,903	CLARE
LIMERICK – BOR	1,477	1,350	1,236	1,167	1,149	1,004	0,736	0,763	28,395	LIMERICK – BOR
LIMERICK – CO	3,775	3,029	2,234	1,852	1,749	1,750	1,300	1,348	55,312	LIMERICK – CO
TIPPERARY – NR	1,705	1,456	1,149	1,211	1,795	1,119	0,806	0,855	27,639	TIPPERARY – NR
CORK – BOR	3,107	3,123	3,156	2,860	2,773	2,453	1,891	2,100	63,710	CORK – BOR
CORK – CO	7,140	7,503	5,677	5,060	5,018	4,723	3,789	3,901	145,038	CORK – CO
KERRY	3,806	3,020	2,534	2,760	2,391	2,345	1,927	2,077	58,451	KERRY
CARLOW	1,279	1,029	0,808	0,768	0,718	0,671	0,520	0,495	20,701	CARLOW
KILKENNY	2,330	1,929	1,503	1,379	1,346	1,257	0,974	0,910	36,052	KILKENNY
TIPPERARY – SR	2,314	1,783	1,527	1,303	1,491	1,367	1,006	1,085	36,567	TIPPERARY – SR
WATERFORD – BOR	1,263	1,131	1,012	0,860	0,717	0,674	0,476	0,547	22,479	WATERFORD – BOR
WATERFORD – CO	1,538	1,324	0,997	0,863	0,899	0,896	0,655	0,650	24,358	WATERFORD – CO
WEXFORD	3,120	2,696	2,150	1,943	1,995	1,785	1,330	1,423	50,418	WEXFORD
DUBLIN – BOR	2,949	9,453	10,472	10,753	11,268	10,206	7,556	8,579	185,890	DUBLIN – BOR
DUN LAOIRE	1,363	1,438	1,404	1,347	1,356	1,217	1,040	1,245	26,697	DUN LAOIRE
DUBLIN – CO	22,857	16,575	11,926	8,544	7,037	5,494	3,942	3,684	357,708	DUBLIN – CO
KILDARE	4,811	3,457	2,312	1,710	1,517	1,409	1,022	0,980	69,140	KILDARE
WICKLOW	3,770	2,950	2,154	1,768	1,669	1,462	1,155	1,287	54,900	WICKLOW
MEATH	3,802	3,016	2,122	1,768	1,641	1,465	1,095	1,067	60,374	MEATH
CAVAN	1,452	1,111	0,967	1,006	1,036	1,061	0,832	0,788	22,603	CAVAN
LOUTH	2,999	2,403	1,926	1,678	1,672	1,665	1,206	1,159	48,330	LOUTH
MONAGHAN	1,596	1,202	1,000	0,923	0,936	0,894	0,677	0,717	25,708	MONAGHAN
LAOIS	1,460	1,243	0,996	0,957	0,960	0,864	0,658	0,665	26,125	LAOIS
LONGFORD	1,014	0,753	0,578	0,582	0,667	0,619	0,480	0,460	15,201	LONGFORD
OFFALY	1,758	1,425	1,208	1,082	1,202	1,022	0,733	0,714	28,590	OFFALY
ROSCOMMON	1,494	1,312	1,067	1,077	1,205	1,104	0,876	0,941	24,628	ROSCOMMON
WESTMEATH	2,022	1,575	1,333	1,167	1,195	1,130	0,768	0,746	31,997	WESTMEATH

REGIONS										REGIONS
DONEGAL	1,846	3,186	2,665	2,229	2,363	2,292	1,947	2,175	66,909	DONEGAL
NORTHWEST	2,571	1,932	1,724	1,549	1,730	1,736	1,397	1,490	39,714	NORTHWEST
WEST	9,061	7,134	5,840	5,212	5,572	5,430	4,553	5,014	142,935	WEST
MIDWEST	10,210	8,288	6,550	5,802	5,767	5,412	4,042	4,266	158,249	MIDWEST
SOUTHWEST	16,662	13,726	11,367	10,177	10,142	9,521	7,607	8,087	267,229	SOUTHWEST
SOUTHEAST	16,344	9,704	7,997	7,297	7,079	6,650	4,961	5,110	192,575	SOUTHEAST
EAST	45,552	36,880	30,300	25,850	24,488	21,253	15,810	16,837	754,209	EAST
NORTHEAST	5,957	4,716	3,893	3,607	3,644	3,620	2,715	2,664	96,641	NORTHEAST
MIDLANDS	7,757	6,228	5,174	4,877	5,207	4,739	3,515	3,526	126,541	MIDLANDS
STATE	113,702	92,303	75,600	66,600	65,888	60,653	46,547	49,160	1,845,002	STATE

COUNTIES	AGED 0-4	AGED 5-9	AGED 10-14	AGED 15-19	AGED 20-24	AGED 25-29	AGED 30-34	AGED 35-39	AGED 40-44
DONEGAL	9,664	11,250	14,175	13,092	10,348	9,157	8,774	8,052	8,653
LEITRIM	1,294	1,623	2,353	2,105	1,375	1,119	1,361	1,512	1,650
SLIGO	3,779	4,318	5,287	5,163	3,436	3,618	3,992	3,977	4,136
GALWAY	12,777	13,181	16,501	17,350	14,261	12,825	13,514	13,105	12,668
MAYO	6,620	8,234	11,161	10,532	7,202	5,554	6,028	6,517	7,792
CLARE	6,604	7,065	8,706	9,339	7,160	6,361	6,504	6,479	6,773
LIMERICK – BOR	4,312	4,079	4,512	4,351	4,623	4,868	5,310	4,397	3,090
LIMERICK – CO	7,450	8,302	10,273	10,047	8,025	7,030	8,321	8,385	8,637
TIPPERARY – NR	3,416	3,711	5,163	5,333	4,137	3,851	4,077	3,807	3,712
CORK – BOR	20,032	8,352	8,602	8,092	10,497	11,730	12,416	10,383	6,411
CORK – CO	7,553	23,015	28,371	28,330	26,150	20,744	20,613	21,172	21,770
KERRY	2,951	8,015	11,306	11,177	6,715	7,530	7,958	7,896	8,503
CARLOW	5,363	3,106	3,003	3,964	3,291	3,029	3,328	3,237	2,892
KILKENNY	5,432	5,363	7,790	7,363	5,564	5,278	5,501	5,576	5,481
TIPPERARY – SR	3,671	6,158	7,542	7,363	5,620	5,205	5,746	5,141	5,259
WATERFORD – BOR	3,317	3,800	3,051	3,000	3,642	3,726	3,673	2,962	2,435
WATERFORD – CO	7,119	3,720	4,592	4,042	3,642	3,544	3,706	3,312	3,517
WEXFORD	18,092	7,714	9,812	7,701	7,753	7,510	7,490	7,061	6,741
DUBLIN – BOR	3,365	10,571	12,389	16,863	31,991	36,321	37,966	32,313	13,560
DUN LAOIRE	63,300	2,991	3,276	3,086	3,607	4,153	4,530	3,773	2,520
DUBLIN – CO	11,379	70,691	72,922	68,019	54,574	55,359	50,286	56,676	55,467
KILDARE		12,329	14,415	13,503	11,656	11,090	11,622	11,532	11,304
WICKLOW	9,736	9,004	10,441	10,119	7,807	7,897	8,175	8,003	7,800
MEATH	2,767	11,152	13,187	12,420	8,616	8,832	9,017	8,753	8,959
CAVAN	7,384	3,241	4,600	4,540	3,223	2,860	3,243	3,328	3,321
LOUTH	3,013	7,578	6,761	8,709	7,657	7,731	7,567	6,948	6,127
MONAGHAN	4,142	4,623	5,400	5,347	3,843	3,580	3,735	3,613	3,541
LAOIS	2,063	4,774	5,627	5,258	3,017	3,881	4,069	3,804	3,672
LONGFORD	4,357	2,305	3,020	3,556	2,119	1,977	2,161	2,141	2,276
OFFALY	3,375	4,015	5,717	5,767	4,533	4,123	4,506	3,977	3,819
ROSCOMMON	4,229	4,355	5,427	4,070	3,170	2,692	2,823	3,061	3,468
WESTMEATH		4,692	6,267	6,236	3,041	4,700	5,023	4,707	4,694

REGIONS	AGED 0-4	AGED 5-9	AGED 10-14	AGED 15-19	AGED 20-24	AGED 25-29	AGED 30-34	AGED 35-39	AGED 40-44
DONEGAL	9,664	11,250	4,175	13,092	10,348	9,157	8,774	8,052	8,653
NORTHWEST	5,063	5,942	7,640	7,268	5,311	4,737	5,353	5,489	5,795
WEST	19,667	21,418	27,745	27,882	21,463	18,379	19,542	19,622	20,460
MIDWEST	22,072	24,060	29,651	29,070	24,771	23,019	24,212	23,068	22,207
SOUTHWEST	37,201	39,215	48,360	46,609	41,352	40,013	41,987	39,451	36,587
SOUTHEAST	28,364	31,227	37,620	37,186	29,428	28,292	29,444	27,289	26,320
EAST	114,617	116,637	126,620	125,000	119,094	123,652	130,596	121,050	99,605
NORTHEAST	14,004	15,445	18,761	18,605	14,723	14,180	14,545	13,889	12,989
MIDLANDS	18,179	20,931	26,060	25,287	18,718	17,373	18,582	17,690	17,929

	AGED 0-4	AGED 5-9	AGED 10-14	AGED 15-19	AGED 20-24	AGED 25-29	AGED 30-34	AGED 35-39	AGED 40-44
STATE	267,751	287,155	336,641	333,900	286,128	278,802	293,035	275,600	250,645

117

1996 CONTINUED

COUNTIES	AGED 45-49	AGED 50-54	AGED 55-59	AGED 60-64	AGED 65-69	AGED 70-74	AGED 75-79	AGED 80+	ALL AGES
DONEGAL	8,105	6,040	5,550	4,687	4,816	4,376	3,581	3,719	136,129
LEITRIM	1,511	1,213	1,151	1,079	1,197	1,097	939	882	23,466
SLIGO	3,847	2,875	2,429	2,136	2,303	2,072	1,596	1,632	57,118
GALWAY	11,728	9,488	7,674	6,488	6,350	5,751	4,534	4,662	187,243
MAYO	7,313	5,756	4,754	4,382	4,615	4,449	3,766	3,795	108,470
CLARE	6,710	5,171	4,073	3,307	3,308	2,893	2,128	2,107	97,055
LIMERICK – BOR	2,301	2,621	2,480	2,236	2,001	1,724	1,128	1,056	55,865
LIMERICK – CO	7,788	6,273	4,604	3,670	3,562	3,147	2,293	2,112	112,823
TIPPERARY – NR	3,502	2,868	2,327	2,346	2,251	2,074	1,468	1,376	55,165
CORK – BOR	6,156	6,030	5,095	5,411	4,927	4,049	2,815	2,791	124,549
CORK – CO	19,956	15,388	11,723	10,082	9,625	8,546	6,610	6,208	295,678
KERRY	7,991	6,461	5,359	4,730	4,811	4,400	3,510	3,481	120,667
CARLOW	2,599	2,104	1,708	1,487	1,377	1,199	834	730	41,738
KILKENNY	4,834	3,048	3,063	2,693	2,657	2,344	1,696	1,471	77,787
TIPPERARY – SR	4,777	3,623	3,151	2,610	2,637	2,527	1,750	1,654	76,674
WATERFORD – BOR	2,413	2,235	1,978	1,681	1,356	1,152	756	755	44,062
WATERFORD – CO	3,189	2,643	2,129	1,920	1,773	1,648	1,169	1,030	49,788
WEXFORD	6,363	5,481	4,489	3,776	3,633	3,199	2,280	2,271	102,460
DUBLIN – BOR	16,568	17,825	19,431	19,608	19,701	16,706	11,452	11,580	343,833
DUN LAOIRE	2,536	2,571	2,471	2,335	2,204	1,944	1,486	1,666	49,584
DUBLIN – CO	45,636	32,655	23,318	16,444	12,821	9,347	6,290	5,230	708,552
KILDARE	9,203	7,122	4,719	3,465	2,912	2,521	1,757	1,503	142,929
WICKLOW	7,486	5,832	4,314	3,451	3,073	2,578	1,911	1,936	108,817
MEATH	8,102	6,282	4,385	3,465	3,161	2,700	1,906	1,707	123,389
CAVAN	3,361	2,420	2,021	2,092	2,175	1,990	1,531	1,326	47,791
LOUTH	5,776	4,862	3,872	3,231	3,079	2,874	1,958	1,730	95,787
MONAGHAN	3,288	2,511	2,060	1,880	1,804	1,708	1,259	1,166	53,342
LAOIS	3,055	2,553	2,069	1,884	2,216	1,689	1,245	1,107	54,649
LONGFORD	2,009	1,577	1,233	1,241	1,245	1,143	850	747	31,262
OFFALY	3,591	2,903	2,442	2,197	2,102	1,920	1,377	1,183	59,241
ROSCOMMON	3,062	2,584	2,277	2,257	2,133	2,125	1,616	1,643	51,388
WESTMEATH	4,155	3,255	2,689	2,366	2,272	2,050	1,361	1,207	64,844

REGIONS	AGED 45-49	AGED 50-54	AGED 55-59	AGED 60-64	AGED 65-69	AGED 70-74	AGED 75-79	AGED 80+	ALL AGES
DONEGAL	8,105	6,040	5,550	4,687	4,816	4,376	3,581	3,719	136,129
NORTHWEST	5,358	4,094	3,580	3,215	3,500	3,169	2,535	2,514	80,584
WEST	19,041	15,244	12,428	10,870	10,965	10,200	8,300	8,457	290,713
MIDWEST	20,295	16,939	13,574	11,768	11,212	10,838	7,101	6,741	321,208
SOUTHWEST	34,103	27,970	23,067	20,235	19,366	16,995	12,065	12,480	540,894
SOUTHEAST	24,201	20,104	16,509	14,408	13,613	12,069	8,485	7,920	392,509
EAST	90,229	72,423	58,671	48,768	44,095	35,805	24,712	23,631	1,476,094
NORTHEAST	12,425	9,796	7,953	7,215	7,058	6,572	4,748	4,222	196,920
MIDLANDS	15,872	12,872	10,710	9,945	9,968	8,927	6,449	5,887	261,379
STATE	230,318	186,291	152,042	131,111	124,613	107,951	78,876	75,571	3,696,430

118

ESTIMATED POPULATION, 2001

MALES

COUNTIES	AGED 0-4	AGED 5-9	AGED 10-14	AGED 15-19	AGED 20-24	AGED 25-29	AGED 30-34	AGED 35-39	AGED 40-44
DONEGAL	5,271	5,450	5,954	6,544	5,564	4,819	4,933	4,695	4,228
LEITRIM	0.633	0.715	0.832	0.986	0.763	0.595	0.621	0.731	0.799
SLIGO	1,985	2,067	2,289	2,519	2,087	1,714	1,943	2,069	2,003
GALWAY	6,303	6,404	7,037	8,121	7,006	6,470	6,706	7,012	6,619
MAYO	3,341	3,774	4,299	4,807	3,747	2,907	3,028	3,360	3,611
CLARE	3,779	3,879	4,274	4,597	3,597	3,678	3,666	3,616	3,508
LIMERICK – BOR	2,086	1,844	1,895	1,960	1,732	2,077	2,293	2,416	2,222
LIMERICK – CO	4,052	4,017	4,396	4,017	3,602	4,423	4,503	4,562	4,440
TIPPERARY – NR	1,701	1,687	1,804	2,206	2,075	1,999	1,965	2,067	1,980
CORK – BOR	1,411	1,900	3,826	3,892	3,949	4,816	5,407	5,941	5,010
CORK – CO	11,024	11,150	12,179	13,118	12,640	11,551	11,727	11,867	11,123
KERRY	3,014	4,116	4,555	5,226	4,625	4,056	4,140	4,333	4,227
CARLOW	1,573	1,632	1,582	1,791	1,625	1,608	1,876	1,676	1,601
KILKENNY	3,102	3,251	3,506	3,673	2,003	2,843	2,878	2,930	2,896
TIPPERARY – SR	2,763	2,854	3,230	3,296	2,671	2,790	3,030	3,287	2,759
WATERFORD – BOR	1,962	1,889	1,965	1,922	1,666	1,786	1,861	1,804	1,363
WATERFORD – CO	1,737	1,734	1,872	2,087	2,011	1,786	1,955	1,934	1,725
WEXFORD	3,789	3,656	3,939	4,484	3,923	3,878	4,084	3,912	3,641
DUBLIN – BOR	7,168	3,060	2,503	5,049	7,645	11,235	10,904	14,348	13,574
DUN LAOIRE	1,614	1,354	1,337	1,496	1,272	1,521	1,665	1,882	1,635
DUBLIN – CO	16,406	37,212	38,533	35,771	31,295	30,803	32,714	31,555	28,496
KILDARE	6,400	6,202	6,769	7,304	6,408	6,617	6,546	6,516	5,988
WICKLOW	4,514	4,490	4,759	4,808	5,243	4,386	4,260	4,287	4,020
MEATH	5,447	5,589	6,029	6,416	5,327	5,045	5,069	5,018	4,611
CAVAN	1,382	1,538	1,656	2,045	1,748	1,559	1,620	1,751	1,824
LOUTH	3,964	3,637	3,846	4,112	3,636	3,707	3,738	3,751	3,350
MONAGHAN	2,070	2,201	2,496	2,508	2,294	2,014	1,900	2,055	1,882
LAOIS	2,105	2,312	2,384	2,689	2,231	1,097	2,226	2,232	1,996
LONGFORD	1,554	1,689	1,204	1,400	1,097	1,076	1,079	1,195	1,080
OFFALY	2,227	2,321	2,473	2,684	2,348	2,206	2,254	2,449	2,118
ROSCOMMON	1,604	1,992	2,261	2,323	1,835	1,424	1,657	1,600	1,697
WESTMEATH	2,265	2,218	2,459	2,892	2,488	2,291	2,604	2,741	2,470

REGIONS	AGED 0-4	AGED 5-9	AGED 10-14	AGED 15-19	AGED 20-24	AGED 25-29	AGED 30-34	AGED 35-39	AGED 40-44
DONEGAL	5,271	5,450	5,954	6,544	5,564	4,819	4,933	4,695	4,228
NORTHWEST	2,618	2,782	3,121	3,505	2,750	2,309	2,564	2,800	2,802
WEST	9,734	10,178	11,336	12,928	10,843	9,386	9,734	10,372	10,230
MIDWEST	11,530	11,427	12,319	13,580	12,277	12,177	12,427	12,661	12,150
SOUTHWEST	19,379	19,215	20,560	22,436	20,654	20,423	21,274	22,141	20,360
SOUTHEAST	14,324	14,876	17,753	17,753	15,228	14,594	15,106	15,543	13,985
EAST	61,660	57,906	59,930	60,924	56,190	59,607	61,158	63,606	58,324
NORTHEAST	7,416	7,336	7,886	8,665	7,678	7,263	7,258	7,654	7,064
MIDLANDS	9,595	6,932	10,893	11,097	10,171	9,011	9,820	10,226	9,361
STATE	142,115	130,111	148,093	158,332	141,305	139,589	144,574	149,698	138,504

119.

2001 CONTINUED

COUNTIES	AGED 45-49	AGED 50-54	AGED 55-59	AGED 60-64	AGED 65-69	AGED 70-74	AGED 75-79	AGED 80+	ALL AGES	COUNTIES
DONEGAL	4,456	4,268	3,613	2,713	2,397	2,038	1,487	1,468	69,897	DONEGAL
LEITRIM	0,785	0,759	0,611	0,560	0,508	0,431	0,351	0,308	11,159	LEITRIM
SLIGO	2,016	1,961	1,447	1,332	1,032	0,931	0,620	0,575	28,290	SLIGO
GALWAY	6,350	5,910	4,723	3,689	2,561	1,979	1,461	1,461	91,936	GALWAY
MAYO	3,980	3,833	2,900	2,367	1,979	1,325	0,951	0,856	53,222	MAYO
CLARE	3,420	3,343	2,577	2,044	1,325	0,856	0,287	0,287	50,860	CLARE
LIMERICK – BOR	1,512	1,437	1,185	0,994	0,701	0,450	0,451	0,450	26,138	LIMERICK – BOR
LIMERICK – CO	4,446	3,944	3,068	2,241	1,855	0,907	0,627	0,761	58,400	LIMERICK – CO
TIPPERARY – NR	1,792	1,710	1,311	1,064	1,035	0,847	0,557	0,557	28,877	TIPPERARY – NR
CORK – BOR	3,215	2,865	2,525	2,525	2,254	1,645	0,686	0,686	58,083	CORK – BOR
CORK – CO	10,751	9,870	7,365	7,339	3,623	3,623	2,268	2,268	152,740	CORK – CO
KERRY	4,370	4,040	3,295	2,600	2,363	1,935	1,335	1,335	60,524	KERRY
CARLOW	1,471	1,264	1,012	0,802	0,631	0,515	0,340	0,237	20,857	CARLOW
KILKENNY	2,605	2,437	1,923	1,477	1,211	1,031	0,704	0,567	40,054	KILKENNY
TIPPERARY – SR	2,729	2,355	1,894	1,477	1,259	1,029	0,755	0,561	39,456	TIPPERARY – SR
WATERFORD – BOR	1,237	1,157	0,810	0,711	0,748	0,692	0,325	0,215	22,223	WATERFORD – BOR
WATERFORD – CO	1,689	1,594	1,240	1,026	0,863	0,691	0,377	0,377	24,811	WATERFORD – CO
WEXFORD	3,399	3,167	2,623	2,161	1,600	1,405	0,964	1,289	51,540	WEXFORD
DUBLIN – BOR	5,471	6,720	7,484	7,739	7,630	6,302	4,139	2,951	123,931	DUBLIN – BOR
DUN LAOIRE	1,176	1,116	1,116	0,964	0,732	0,485	0,303	0,303	20,568	DUN LAOIRE
KILDARE	5,663	5,016	3,543	2,194	1,595	1,111	0,563	0,563	56,440	KILDARE
DUBLIN – CO	27,242	22,474	15,393	10,529	4,669	4,139	1,794	1,794	395,025	DUBLIN – CO
WICKLOW	3,894	3,709	2,799	2,021	1,618	1,127	0,769	0,656	79,098	WICKLOW
MEATH	4,430	4,127	3,119	2,055	1,560	1,206	0,839	0,656	66,594	MEATH
CAVAN	1,656	1,542	1,213	1,006	1,206	0,896	0,684	0,517	23,549	CAVAN
LOUTH	3,106	2,760	2,312	1,779	1,415	1,045	0,623	0,600	47,634	LOUTH
MONAGHAN	1,789	1,514	1,220	1,006	1,045	0,744	0,799	0,517	27,424	MONAGHAN
LAOIS	1,827	1,623	1,249	0,872	0,871	0,720	0,562	0,435	28,524	LAOIS
LONGFORD	1,163	1,048	0,908	0,847	0,744	0,443	0,338	0,443	15,646	LONGFORD
OFFALY	1,871	1,695	1,370	0,976	0,896	0,613	0,613	0,500	30,146	OFFALY
ROSCOMMON	1,789	1,539	1,303	0,910	1,007	0,690	0,642	0,642	25,653	ROSCOMMON
WESTMEATH	2,359	2,076	1,582	1,246	1,064	0,837	0,628	0,463	32,683	WESTMEATH

REGIONS	AGED 45-49	AGED 50-54	AGED 55-59	AGED 60-64	AGED 65-69	AGED 70-74	AGED 75-79	AGED 80+	ALL AGES	REGIONS
DONEGAL	4,456	4,268	3,613	2,713	2,397	2,038	1,487	1,468	69,897	DONEGAL
NORTHWEST	2,801	2,720	2,058	1,602	1,539	1,439	0,971	0,938	39,449	NORTHWEST
WEST	10,330	9,743	7,713	6,056	5,412	4,540	3,374	3,240	145,158	WEST
MIDWEST	11,170	10,443	8,141	6,346	5,475	4,236	2,944	2,431	161,813	MIDWEST
SOUTHWEST	18,339	16,775	13,337	10,673	9,270	7,203	5,019	4,289	271,347	SOUTHWEST
SOUTHEAST	13,220	11,971	10,645	7,770	6,418	5,153	3,572	2,777	198,941	SOUTHEAST
EAST	47,920	43,092	33,381	25,492	20,601	15,147	9,624	7,005	741,656	EAST
NORTHEAST	6,551	5,331	4,745	3,693	3,258	2,685	1,974	1,547	98,607	NORTHEAST
MIDLANDS	9,004	7,872	6,258	5,065	4,614	3,827	2,831	2,325	132,652	MIDLANDS
STATE	123,791	112,821	88,891	69,509	59,094	46,268	31,796	26,029	1,859,520	STATE

120

COUNTIES	AGED 0-4	AGED 5-9	AGED 10-14	AGED 15-19	AGED 20-24	AGED 25-29	AGED 30-34	AGED 35-39	AGED 40-44	COUNTIES
DONEGAL	5,010	5,334	5,793	6,356	5,247	4,556	4,532	4,418	3,980	DONEGAL
LEITRIM	0,561	0,651	0,740	0,957	0,588	0,440	0,534	0,639	0,693	LEITRIM
SLIGO	1,820	1,924	2,144	2,258	1,931	1,784	1,921	2,076	2,061	SLIGO
GALWAY	6,005	6,238	6,605	7,330	6,768	6,268	6,446	6,916	6,684	GALWAY
MAYO	3,152	3,553	4,098	4,707	3,406	2,535	2,823	3,007	3,053	MAYO
CLARE	3,477	3,613	3,968	4,119	3,377	3,130	3,271	3,182	3,121	CLARE
LIMERICK – BOR	1,750	1,749	1,792	2,172	1,816	1,974	2,078	2,490	1,917	LIMERICK – BOR
LIMERICK – CO	3,851	3,816	4,153	4,591	4,182	4,119	4,095	4,205	4,150	LIMERICK – CO
TIPPERARY – NR	1,700	1,648	1,847	2,251	1,832	1,705	1,870	1,988	1,740	TIPPERARY – NR
CORK – BOR	4,162	3,725	3,682	3,748	4,130	4,629	4,919	5,596	4,824	CORK – BOR
CORK – CO	10,391	10,485	11,378	12,203	10,583	10,123	10,686	10,605	10,229	CORK – CO
KERRY	3,673	3,870	4,380	4,673	3,920	3,487	3,658	3,757	3,760	KERRY
CARLOW	1,423	1,772	1,449	1,667	1,454	1,479	1,550	1,712	1,602	CARLOW
KILKENNY	2,004	3,032	3,292	3,274	2,704	2,414	2,657	2,693	2,709	KILKENNY
TIPPERARY – SR	2,610	2,567	2,916	2,995	2,401	2,188	2,267	2,481	2,402	TIPPERARY – SR
WATERFORD – BOR	1,841	1,904	1,880	1,874	1,707	1,722	1,730	1,775	1,568	WATERFORD – BOR
WATERFORD – CO	1,641	1,654	1,796	1,722	1,708	1,615	1,686	1,789	1,540	WATERFORD – CO
WEXFORD	3,521	3,442	3,725	4,160	3,525	3,387	3,577	3,614	3,405	WEXFORD
DUBLIN – BOR	6,474	2,606	2,215	5,899	11,560	12,239	11,578	16,439	14,982	DUBLIN – BOR
DUN LAOIRE	1,523	1,279	1,268	1,727	1,568	1,707	1,839	2,342	2,010	DUN LAOIRE
DUBLIN – CO	34,228	35,222	36,616	34,167	30,473	31,650	33,468	32,681	29,912	DUBLIN – CO
KILDARE	4,330	5,795	6,185	6,309	4,100	5,836	5,851	5,878	5,165	KILDARE
WICKLOW	3,978	4,228	4,588	4,771	3,410	4,271	4,415	4,356	4,421	WICKLOW
MEATH	5,141	5,277	5,665	5,813	4,894	4,598	4,676	4,622	4,421	MEATH
CAVAN	1,251	1,314	1,463	1,840	1,399	1,584	1,286	1,368	1,415	CAVAN
LOUTH	3,673	3,445	3,600	3,739	3,632	3,739	3,460	3,739	3,463	LOUTH
MONAGHAN	1,941	2,051	2,233	2,307	1,877	1,581	1,707	1,887	1,697	MONAGHAN
LAOIS	2,024	2,149	2,255	2,297	1,829	1,652	1,770	1,887	1,781	LAOIS
LONGFORD	1,026	1,006	1,127	1,275	0,995	0,824	1,031	1,067	1,069	LONGFORD
OFFALY	2,100	2,125	2,242	2,389	1,942	1,834	1,932	2,050	1,818	OFFALY
ROSCOMMON	1,610	1,918	2,170	2,306	1,400	1,028	1,146	1,322	1,391	ROSCOMMON
WESTMEATH	2,082	2,115	2,380	2,784	2,288	2,210	2,325	2,408	2,296	WESTMEATH
REGIONS										REGIONS
DONEGAL	5,010	5,334	5,793	6,356	5,247	4,556	4,532	4,418	3,980	DONEGAL
NORTHWEST	2,381	2,575	2,884	3,215	2,519	2,233	2,455	2,715	2,754	NORTHWEST
WEST	9,157	9,591	10,703	12,176	10,174	8,803	9,269	9,923	9,737	WEST
MIDWEST	10,978	10,826	11,760	13,133	11,207	10,937	11,323	11,866	10,928	MIDWEST
SOUTHWEST	18,216	18,080	19,449	21,114	18,633	18,239	19,263	19,958	18,813	SOUTHWEST
SOUTHEAST	13,016	13,961	15,067	15,892	13,409	12,805	13,517	14,064	13,226	SOUTHEAST
EAST	57,743	54,197	56,537	58,686	56,705	60,901	61,777	66,311	61,364	EAST
NORTHEAST	6,865	6,810	7,296	7,986	6,209	6,424	6,853	6,819	6,575	NORTHEAST
MIDLANDS	8,842	9,313	10,174	11,050	8,544	7,548	8,204	8,734	8,355	MIDLANDS
STATE	133,138	130,987	139,663	149,608	133,436	132,446	137,143	144,808	135,736	STATE

FEMALES

2001 CONTINUED

COUNTIES	AGED 45-49	AGED 50-54	AGED 55-59	AGED 60-64	AGED 65-69	AGED 70-74	AGED 75-79	AGED 80+	ALL AGES	COUNTIES
DONEGAL	4,201	4,032	3,119	2,594	2,212	2,134	1,844	2,225	67,587	DONEGAL
LEITRIM	0,821	0,713	0,565	0,497	0,504	0,501	0,433	0,497	10,343	LEITRIM
SLIGO	2,064	1,801	1,325	1,172	1,016	1,047	0,919	1,045	28,308	SLIGO
GALWAY	6,317	5,612	4,376	3,442	3,193	2,949	2,446	2,906	90,340	GALWAY
MAYO	3,741	3,333	2,522	2,120	2,088	2,063	1,873	2,295	50,459	MAYO
CLARE	3,310	3,236	2,392	1,822	1,558	1,455	1,179	1,350	47,569	CLARE
LIMERICK – BOR	1,435	1,411	1,266	1,149	1,111	0,991	0,778	0,788	26,866	LIMERICK – BOR
LIMERICK – CO	1,419	3,732	2,030	2,123	1,795	1,557	1,357	1,425	56,309	LIMERICK – CO
TIPPERARY – NR	2,842	3,022	2,973	2,012	1,751	2,398	0,916	0,000	26,574	TIPPERARY – NR
CORK – BOR	2,842	3,721	2,953	2,402	2,204	2,142	1,827	2,165	60,656	CORK – BOR
CORK – CO	10,847	9,542	7,380	5,416	4,977	4,404	3,713	4,147	147,189	CORK – CO
KERRY	4,045	3,721	2,973	2,751	2,204	2,398	1,971	2,111	56,792	KERRY
CARLOW	1,401	1,239	1,009	0,774	0,751	0,615	0,538	0,545	20,589	CARLOW
KILKENNY	2,713	2,298	1,873	1,153	1,325	1,182	0,967	1,009	38,499	KILKENNY
TIPPERARY – SR	2,436	2,276	1,714	1,435	1,329	1,259	1,062	1,135	35,573	TIPPERARY – SR
WATERFORD – BOR	1,211	1,253	1,116	0,968	0,836	0,671	0,550	0,562	23,117	WATERFORD – BOR
WATERFORD – CO	1,747	1,501	1,219	0,931	0,738	0,762	0,670	0,685	23,860	WATERFORD – CO
WEXFORD	3,279	3,105	2,635	2,067	1,874	1,653	1,412	1,497	49,879	WEXFORD
DUBLIN – BOR	5,943	8,114	8,367	9,445	8,805	9,538	7,914	8,706	151,520	DUBLIN – BOR
DUN LAOIRE	1,257	1,333	1,367	1,357	1,308	1,215	0,986	1,280	75,368	DUN LAOIRE
DUBLIN – CO	28,563	22,786	16,347	11,612	8,643	6,450	4,601	4,437	401,916	DUBLIN – CO
KILDARE	5,630	4,809	3,341	2,188	1,661	1,356	1,106	1,098	74,301	KILDARE
WICKLOW	4,024	3,690	2,897	2,054	1,698	1,517	1,203	1,393	57,708	WICKLOW
MEATH	4,506	3,848	2,819	2,009	1,762	1,432	1,149	1,180	63,942	MEATH
CAVAN	1,568	1,401	1,074	0,901	0,989	0,878	0,805	0,845	20,901	CAVAN
LOUTH	2,931	2,838	2,358	1,855	1,632	1,478	1,304	1,316	48,702	LOUTH
MONAGHAN	1,605	1,556	1,138	0,930	0,891	0,818	0,620	0,731	25,564	MONAGHAN
LAOIS	1,758	1,441	1,190	0,955	0,905	0,855	0,678	0,710	26,136	LAOIS
LONGFORD	1,077	0,992	0,732	0,560	0,578	0,578	0,478	0,501	14,917	LONGFORD
OFFALY	1,803	1,706	1,304	1,135	1,031	0,920	0,800	0,804	28,114	OFFALY
ROSCOMMON	1,608	1,459	1,187	0,998	1,056	1,057	0,836	0,968	23,549	ROSCOMMON
WESTMEATH	2,297	1,901	1,550	1,243	1,130	1,046	0,895	0,801	31,850	WESTMEATH

REGIONS	AGED 45-49	AGED 50-54	AGED 55-59	AGED 60-64	AGED 65-69	AGED 70-74	AGED 75-79	AGED 80+	ALL AGES	REGIONS
DONEGAL	4,201	4,032	3,119	2,594	2,212	2,134	1,844	2,225	67,587	DONEGAL
NORTHWEST	2,885	2,514	1,800	1,660	1,520	1,548	1,352	1,542	38,651	NORTHWEST
WEST	10,058	8,945	6,892	5,562	5,271	5,012	4,310	5,463	140,799	WEST
MIDWEST	10,783	10,043	8,007	6,204	5,607	5,023	4,230	4,463	157,318	MIDWEST
SOUTHWEST	17,734	16,285	13,306	10,737	9,932	8,944	7,511	8,423	264,637	SOUTHWEST
SOUTHEAST	12,730	11,672	9,622	7,628	7,053	6,147	5,139	5,433	191,516	SOUTHEAST
EAST	47,923	44,588	35,574	28,667	24,967	21,508	16,959	16,959	774,755	EAST
NORTHEAST	6,134	5,735	4,570	3,695	3,512	3,174	2,799	2,892	95,167	NORTHEAST
MIDLANDS	8,633	7,588	6,062	4,891	4,700	4,456	3,688	3,784	124,566	MIDLANDS
STATE	123,201	111,462	89,048	71,647	64,774	57,941	47,901	52,057	1,854,996	STATE

122

COUNTIES	AGED 0-4	AGED 5-9	AGED 10-14	AGED 15-19	AGED 20-24	AGED 25-29	AGED 30-34	AGED 35-39	AGED 40-44
DONEGAL	10,281	10,793	11,747	12,900	10,811	9,375	9,465	9,113	8,208
LEITRIM	1,194	1,366	1,572	1,943	1,351	1,044	1,155	1,370	1,492
SLIGO	3,805	3,991	4,433	4,777	3,918	3,498	3,864	4,145	4,064
GALWAY	12,398	12,442	13,642	15,500	13,864	12,747	13,152	13,928	13,303
MAYO	6,403	7,127	8,307	9,604	7,153	5,442	5,851	6,367	6,664
CLARE	7,247	7,192	8,202	8,716	7,245	6,817	6,937	6,798	6,629
LIMERICK – BOR	7,036	3,593	3,677	4,132	3,548	4,051	4,371	4,906	4,139
LIMERICK – CO	7,003	7,833	8,549	9,408	8,784	8,543	8,598	8,767	8,590
TIPPERARY – NR	3,401	3,335	3,651	4,457	3,907	3,704	3,844	4,056	3,720
CORK – BOR	8,603	7,634	7,508	7,840	8,070	9,445	10,326	11,537	9,834
CORK – CO	21,405	21,675	23,557	25,611	22,663	21,674	22,413	22,472	21,352
KERRY	7,597	7,986	8,944	10,000	8,545	7,514	7,798	8,090	7,987
CARLOW	3,002	2,864	3,031	3,153	3,118	3,087	3,149	3,388	3,203
KILKENNY	6,004	6,798	6,798	6,791	5,697	5,257	5,535	5,623	5,605
TIPPERARY – SR	5,373	5,521	6,146	6,796	5,377	4,978	5,297	5,768	5,161
WATERFORD – BOR	3,803	3,683	3,854	4,002	3,373	3,411	3,641	3,570	2,931
WATERFORD – CO	3,378	3,388	3,668	3,644	3,719	3,401	3,641	3,773	3,265
WEXFORD	7,310	7,098	7,664	8,644	7,448	7,265	7,661	7,526	7,046
DUBLIN – BOR	13,642	5,765	4,718	10,048	17,815	24,074	22,482	30,787	28,556
DUN LAOIRE	3,137	2,633	2,605	3,223	2,840	3,228	3,504	4,224	3,645
DUBLIN – CO	70,784	72,134	75,140	69,938	61,768	62,653	66,182	64,236	58,408
KILDARE	12,378	11,997	12,954	13,613	11,818	12,453	12,397	12,387	11,866
WICKLOW	6,883	8,778	9,347	9,650	8,433	8,657	8,575	8,643	8,185
MEATH	10,588	10,866	11,664	12,729	10,221	9,643	9,906	8,640	9,032
CAVAN	2,633	2,752	3,119	3,885	3,147	2,673	2,906	3,216	3,239
LOUTH	7,637	7,142	7,446	7,951	7,268	7,448	7,598	7,490	6,821
MONAGHAN	4,011	4,252	4,617	4,086	4,171	3,668	3,996	3,767	3,579
LAOIS	4,219	4,461	4,751	4,815	4,060	3,666	3,607	4,119	3,777
LONGFORD	2,080	2,095	2,331	2,684	2,214	1,900	2,110	2,262	2,142
OFFALY	4,307	4,146	4,715	5,072	4,200	4,040	4,186	2,409	3,936
ROSCOMMON	3,204	3,910	4,431	4,629	3,325	2,452	2,803	2,931	3,088
WESTMEATH	4,347	4,333	4,939	5,676	4,776	4,501	4,029	5,149	4,766

REGIONS	AGED 0-4	AGED 5-9	AGED 10-14	AGED 15-19	AGED 20-24	AGED 25-29	AGED 30-34	AGED 35-39	AGED 40-44
DONEGAL	10,281	10,793	11,747	12,900	10,811	9,375	9,465	9,113	8,208
NORTHWEST	4,999	5,357	6,005	6,722	5,269	4,542	5,019	5,515	5,556
WEST	18,801	19,760	22,039	26,104	21,017	19,180	19,003	20,295	19,967
MIDWEST	22,587	22,253	24,079	26,713	23,464	23,750	23,750	24,527	23,078
SOUTHWEST	37,595	37,295	40,009	43,550	39,287	38,662	40,537	42,099	39,173
SOUTHEAST	28,870	28,837	31,161	33,645	30,727	27,390	28,023	29,607	27,211
EAST	119,412	112,403	116,467	119,610	112,805	120,508	122,885	129,917	119,692
NORTHEAST	14,412	14,146	15,182	16,651	14,586	13,687	14,111	14,473	13,639
MIDLANDS	18,337	19,245	21,067	23,047	18,665	16,550	18,024	18,960	17,716
STATE	275,253	270,098	287,756	307,940	274,741	272,035	281,717	294,506	274,240

123

COUNTIES	AGED 45-49	AGED 50-54	AGED 55-59	AGED 60-64	AGED 65-69	AGED 70-74	AGED 75-79	AGED 80+	ALL AGES
DONEGAL	8,657	8,300	6,732	5,307	4,599	4,172	3,331	3,693	137,484
LEITRIM	1,606	1,472	1,176	1,057	1,051	1,000	784	860	21,502
SLIGO	4,080	3,762	2,772	2,304	2,018	1,978	1,539	1,620	56,508
GALWAY	12,667	11,522	9,009	7,131	6,340	5,510	4,337	4,604	182,276
MAYO	7,721	7,166	5,512	4,187	4,343	4,042	4,356	3,756	103,681
CLARE	6,730	6,579	4,960	3,766	3,195	2,780	2,130	2,206	98,438
LIMERICK – BOR	2,947	2,849	2,451	2,242	2,059	1,602	1,237	1,075	53,004
LIMERICK – CO	8,665	7,676	2,721	4,367	3,650	2,920	2,264	2,186	114,709
TIPPERARY – NR	3,611	3,383	2,721	2,175	2,178	1,867	1,543	1,427	52,990
CORK – BOR	6,057	5,897	5,650	5,441	5,005	4,043	2,996	2,851	118,730
CORK – CO	21,601	19,412	14,745	10,964	5,567	8,027	6,313	6,415	299,929
KERRY	8,415	7,761	6,249	5,002	4,567	4,077	3,221	3,446	117,316
CARLOW	2,875	2,503	2,021	1,576	1,392	1,130	878	782	41,446
KILKENNY	5,408	4,735	3,796	2,646	2,556	2,213	1,671	1,576	78,553
TIPPERARY – SR	5,165	4,631	3,518	2,912	2,598	2,288	1,817	1,703	75,029
WATERFORD – BOR	2,448	2,410	2,159	1,862	1,535	1,153	875	777	45,340
WATERFORD – CO	3,436	3,095	2,515	1,957	1,807	1,453	1,154	1,062	48,671
WEXFORD	6,678	6,272	5,258	4,231	3,573	3,058	2,376	2,310	101,418
DUBLIN – BOR	11,414	14,334	16,157	17,184	17,525	15,840	12,053	11,657	275,451
DUN LAOIRE	2,133	2,449	2,410	2,323	2,191	1,947	1,471	1,673	45,936
DUBLIN – CO	55,805	45,260	31,740	22,341	16,032	11,105	7,255	6,231	796,941
KILDARE	11,228	9,754	6,884	4,372	3,256	2,467	1,844	1,661	153,399
WICKLOW	7,895	7,198	5,696	4,075	3,316	2,644	1,972	2,049	114,148
MEATH	8,995	7,075	6,068	4,064	3,322	2,638	1,988	1,828	130,536
CAVAN	3,224	2,943	2,287	1,960	1,960	1,774	1,428	1,357	44,450
LOUTH	6,237	5,607	4,670	3,634	3,047	2,523	2,103	1,916	96,336
MONAGHAN	3,484	3,179	2,358	2,347	1,763	1,562	1,242	1,166	52,988
LAOIS	3,580	2,955	2,439	1,731	1,752	1,575	1,240	1,153	54,660
LONGFORD	2,240	2,040	1,486	1,165	1,191	1,021	817	778	30,563
OFFALY	3,764	3,401	2,764	2,263	2,030	1,740	1,413	1,304	59,260
ROSCOMMON	3,397	2,997	2,490	2,108	2,147	2,064	1,526	1,610	49,202
WESTMEATH	4,656	4,057	3,141	2,480	2,104	1,883	1,523	1,264	64,533

REGIONS	AGED 45-49	AGED 50-54	AGED 55-59	AGED 60-64	AGED 65-69	AGED 70-74	AGED 75-79	AGED 80+	ALL AGES
DONEGAL	8,657	8,300	6,732	5,307	4,599	4,172	3,331	3,693	137,484
NORTHWEST	5,686	5,234	3,948	3,361	3,099	2,987	2,323	2,480	78,100
WEST	20,388	19,688	14,611	11,614	10,683	9,552	7,693	8,450	285,957
MIDWEST	21,053	20,486	16,148	12,550	11,082	9,250	7,174	6,894	319,131
SOUTHWEST	36,073	31,060	26,643	21,410	19,202	16,147	12,530	12,712	535,984
SOUTHEAST	26,010	23,646	19,267	15,407	13,471	11,295	8,771	8,710	390,457
EAST	97,843	87,680	68,955	54,159	45,648	36,655	26,583	25,099	1,516,411
NORTHEAST	12,745	11,722	9,315	7,388	6,770	5,859	4,773	4,439	193,774
MIDLANDS	17,637	15,460	12,320	9,956	9,314	8,283	6,519	6,109	257,218
STATE	246,992	224,283	177,939	141,156	123,868	104,209	79,697	78,086	3,714,516

ESTIMATED POPULATION, 2006

MALES

COUNTIES	AGED 0-4	AGED 5-9	AGED 10-14	AGED 15-19	AGED 20-24	AGED 25-29	AGED 30-34	AGED 35-39	AGED 40-44
DONEGAL	5,454	5,804	5,724	5,819	5,923	5,235	4,992	5,109	4,791
LEITRIM	0,588	0,673	0,710	0,694	0,783	0,615	0,720	0,602	0,720
SLIGO	1,946	2,001	2,110	2,205	2,210	1,793	1,829	2,029	2,121
GALWAY	6,227	6,600	6,652	7,087	7,493	6,541	7,037	6,888	7,132
MAYO	3,213	3,722	3,832	3,995	3,991	3,021	3,037	3,203	3,474
CLARE	3,822	4,080	3,996	4,136	4,259	3,829	3,939	3,793	3,705
LIMERICK – BOR	1,722	1,700	1,638	1,786	1,831	1,573	1,868	2,096	2,306
LIMERICK – CO	4,158	4,277	4,158	4,340	4,534	4,573	4,719	4,710	4,678
TIPPERARY – NR	1,606	1,686	1,609	1,628	1,637	1,900	1,935	1,938	2,027
CORK – BOR	3,758	3,675	3,454	3,663	3,996	3,691	4,183	4,907	5,664
CORK – CO	11,232	11,535	11,478	11,872	12,631	12,106	12,276	12,093	11,934
KERRY	3,821	4,151	4,119	4,365	4,660	4,180	4,167	4,207	4,373
CARLOW	1,512	1,522	1,456	1,496	1,661	1,596	1,648	1,617	1,660
KILKENNY	3,108	3,336	3,286	3,360	3,405	2,939	2,926	2,920	2,934
TIPPERARY – SR	2,651	2,840	2,201	3,244	3,323	2,764	2,833	3,043	3,304
WATERFORD – BOR	1,922	1,963	1,905	2,091	1,874	1,653	1,674	1,811	1,772
WATERFORD – CO	1,603	1,776	1,705	1,733	1,875	1,927	1,828	1,945	1,904
WEXFORD	3,723	3,766	3,623	3,703	4,100	3,787	4,045	4,045	3,919
DUBLIN – BOR	2,886	0,378	0,030	1,522	6,022	4,550	4,663	7,231	12,408
DUN LAOIRE	1,345	1,243	1,206	1,306	1,430	1,147	1,206	1,491	1,803
DUBLIN – CO	39,893	41,435	39,449	39,148	36,273	35,467	36,362	35,412	32,497
KILDARE	6,781	6,758	6,602	6,604	6,296	6,943	7,225	6,936	6,679
WICKLOW	4,737	4,835	4,614	4,668	4,603	4,471	4,703	4,457	4,368
MEATH	5,772	6,464	5,882	6,020	6,164	5,436	5,472	5,385	5,182
CAVAN	3,994	1,377	1,402	1,501	1,745	1,571	1,539	1,798	1,798
LOUTH	3,994	3,845	3,624	3,711	3,911	3,623	3,616	3,709	3,692
MONAGHAN	2,199	2,243	2,197	2,300	2,350	2,196	1,982	1,909	2,036
LAOIS	1,031	2,357	2,332	2,415	2,492	2,184	2,018	2,229	2,225
LONGFORD	1,031	1,096	1,095	1,151	1,724	1,135	1,108	1,115	1,185
OFFALY	2,232	2,352	2,282	2,377	2,416	2,162	2,209	2,227	2,412
ROSCOMMON	1,656	1,758	2,033	2,058	1,943	1,558	1,422	1,704	1,610
WESTMEATH	2,229	2,292	2,281	2,440	2,600	2,344	2,392	2,666	2,771

REGIONS	AGED 0-4	AGED 5-9	AGED 10-14	AGED 15-19	AGED 20-24	AGED 25-29	AGED 30-34	AGED 35-39	AGED 40-44
DONEGAL	5,454	5,804	5,724	5,819	5,923	5,235	4,992	5,109	4,791
NORTHWEST	2,534	2,761	2,813	3,015	2,993	2,108	2,418	2,631	2,841
WEST	9,536	10,322	10,484	10,982	11,384	9,562	9,589	10,091	10,606
MIDWEST	11,448	11,752	11,401	11,890	12,561	11,875	12,461	12,537	12,716
SOUTHWEST	18,868	19,627	19,051	19,000	21,286	19,979	20,626	21,297	21,971
SOUTHEAST	14,616	15,210	14,876	15,552	16,228	14,666	14,856	15,381	15,502
EAST	61,441	60,713	57,783	59,658	61,938	58,014	59,631	60,592	62,937
NORTHEAST	7,260	7,465	7,223	7,512	8,006	7,390	7,137	7,208	7,526
MIDLANDS	9,338	10,055	10,023	10,441	10,675	9,383	9,149	9,941	10,203

STATE	AGED 0-4	AGED 5-9	AGED 10-14	AGED 15-19	AGED 20-24	AGED 25-29	AGED 30-34	AGED 35-39	AGED 40-44
STATE	140,505	143,719	139,378	144,669	151,014	138,512	140,859	145,107	149,093

125

MALES — 2006 CONTINUED

COUNTIES	AGED 45-49	AGED 50-54	AGED 55-59	AGED 60-64	AGED 65-69	AGED 70-74	AGED 75-79	AGED 80+	ALL AGES
DONEGAL	4.226	4.401	4.098	3.375	2.630	1.999	1.456	1.364	72.400
LEITRIM	0.759	0.751	0.730	0.555	0.608	0.447	0.340	0.301	10.394
SLIGO	1.966	1.072	1.855	1.321	1.074	0.847	0.635	0.520	28.540
GALWAY	6.609	6.187	5.610	4.289	3.513	2.631	1.805	1.683	93.569
MAYO	3.580	3.895	3.643	2.790	2.283	1.943	1.414	1.302	52.181
CLARE	3.425	3.308	3.169	2.338	1.834	1.313	0.912	0.810	52.808
LIMERICK – BOR	2.121	1.442	1.339	1.043	0.973	0.709	0.446	0.320	24.995
LIMERICK – CO	4.152	4.362	3.728	2.797	2.061	1.439	0.884	0.714	60.584
TIPPERARY – NR	1.913	1.715	1.595	1.184	0.973	1.700	0.574	0.511	25.549
CORK – BOR	4.804	3.025	2.637	2.387	2.244	1.700	1.058	0.741	55.667
CORK – CO	10.780	10.390	9.312	6.747	5.152	3.676	2.465	2.137	158.350
KERRY	4.186	4.212	3.860	3.027	2.471	1.896	1.311	1.195	60.220
CARLOW	1.571	1.420	1.199	0.904	0.711	0.487	0.331	0.248	21.072
KILKENNY	2.823	2.612	2.318	1.746	1.301	0.957	0.666	0.559	41.220
TIPPERARY – SR	2.709	2.622	2.223	1.640	1.311	0.958	0.667	0.574	39.597
WATERFORD – BOR	1.364	1.212	1.096	0.964	0.816	0.597	0.328	0.241	23.193
WATERFORD – CO	1.663	1.631	1.499	1.133	0.927	0.683	0.443	0.360	24.737
WEXFORD	3.619	3.312	2.983	2.422	1.901	1.381	0.957	0.808	52.077
DUBLIN – BOR	12.351	4.633	5.926	6.395	6.632	5.623	4.006	3.064	88.320
DUN LAOIRE	1.571	1.112	1.027	0.942	0.865	0.700	3.488	2.404	119.353
DUBLIN – CO	28.537	26.743	21.421	14.167	9.837	5.962	3.203	2.084	447.890
KILDARE	5.965	5.535	4.685	3.217	1.994	1.245	0.737	0.578	86.170
WICKLOW	4.069	3.803	3.517	2.575	1.808	1.302	0.777	0.665	60.152
MEATH	4.628	4.377	3.931	2.833	1.894	1.243	0.814	0.664	71.808
CAVAN	1.755	1.607	1.433	1.104	0.900	0.768	0.601	0.635	22.435
LOUTH	3.298	2.981	2.605	2.111	1.626	1.119	0.688	0.414	48.688
MONAGHAN	1.836	1.717	1.513	1.100	0.895	0.687	0.505	0.446	27.892
LAOIS	1.937	1.749	1.418	1.136	0.822	0.649	0.491	0.256	29.163
LONGFORD	1.072	1.123	0.991	0.688	0.572	0.473	0.284	0.404	15.599
OFFALY	2.203	1.812	1.575	1.252	1.010	0.793	0.560	0.494	30.264
ROSCOMMON	1.665	1.746	1.461	1.195	1.030	0.901	0.681	0.579	25.200
WESTMEATH	2.441	2.294	1.971	1.452	1.111	0.825	0.573	0.482	33.167

REGIONS

COUNTIES	AGED 45-49	AGED 50-54	AGED 55-59	AGED 60-64	AGED 65-69	AGED 70-74	AGED 75-79	AGED 80+	ALL AGES
DONEGAL	4.226	4.401	4.098	3.375	2.630	1.999	1.456	1.364	72.400
NORTHWEST	2.725	2.733	2.585	1.876	1.608	1.294	0.975	1.021	38.934
WEST	10.189	10.062	9.253	7.079	5.796	4.574	3.219	2.985	145.750
MIDWEST	11.984	10.827	9.831	7.362	5.841	4.279	2.816	2.355	163.936
SOUTHWEST	19.770	17.643	15.849	12.161	7.867	7.272	4.837	4.073	274.237
SOUTHEAST	13.751	12.800	11.318	8.800	7.057	5.063	3.392	2.790	201.896
EAST	57.121	46.230	40.507	30.129	23.120	16.075	10.025	7.450	773.693
NORTHEAST	6.889	6.305	5.551	4.315	3.348	2.574	1.794	1.517	99.015
MIDLANDS	9.201	8.731	7.416	5.723	4.627	3.641	2.589	2.257	133.393
STATE	136.056	119.761	106.368	80.829	63.894	46.771	31.103	25.616	1903.254

126

FEMALES   2006 CONTINUED

COUNTIES	AGED 0-4	AGED 5-9	AGED 10-14	AGED 15-19	AGED 20-24	AGED 25-29	AGED 30-34	AGED 35-39	AGED 40-44
DONEGAL	5,188	5,645	5,568	5,592	5,694	4,914	4,698	4,703	4,503
LEITRIM	0,513	0,606	0,620	0,616	0,670	0,447	0,491	0,561	0,634
SLIGO	1,774	1,930	1,986	2,066	2,002	1,809	1,916	1,988	2,124
GALWAY	5,705	6,205	6,248	6,572	6,806	6,257	6,527	6,681	7,035
MAYO	3,057	3,401	3,659	3,705	3,762	2,595	2,704	2,988	3,061
CLARE	3,502	3,703	3,733	3,717	3,618	3,292	3,460	3,444	3,263
LIMERICK – BOR	1,673	1,618	1,554	1,813	2,082	1,566	1,679	1,868	2,355
LIMERICK – CO	3,344	4,041	3,922	4,024	4,220	4,701	4,491	4,340	4,319
TIPPERARY – NR	1,609	1,645	1,662	1,676	1,835	1,663	1,763	1,885	1,954
CORK – BOR	3,518	3,487	3,328	3,615	1,258	3,715	3,839	4,444	5,355
CORK – CO	10,612	11,010	10,715	10,804	11,161	10,752	11,084	11,194	10,781
KERRY	3,500	3,395	3,968	4,050	1,870	3,465	3,638	3,725	3,831
CARLOW	1,375	1,396	1,334	1,353	1,495	1,432	1,559	1,591	1,604
KILKENNY	2,914	3,100	3,077	3,094	3,094	2,626	2,589	2,740	2,737
TIPPERARY – SR	2,507	2,640	2,606	2,654	2,470	2,144	2,236	2,276	2,498
WATERFORD – BOR	1,814	1,866	1,823	1,946	1,706	1,677	1,651	1,736	1,784
WATERFORD – CO	1,602	1,685	1,630	1,653	1,602	1,662	1,670	1,714	1,782
WEXFORD	3,450	3,538	3,426	3,427	3,615	3,417	3,470	3,655	3,613
DUBLIN – BOR	2,460	2,125	2,128	2,702	5,371	6,608	5,452	8,001	14,729
DUN LAOIRE	1,268	1,171	1,143	1,465	1,888	1,355	1,364	1,702	2,304
DUBLIN – CO	37,440	30,088	37,462	37,511	35,530	35,733	37,010	35,780	33,637
KILDARE	6,332	6,289	6,023	6,089	6,325	6,028	6,554	6,234	6,077
WICKLOW	4,527	4,554	4,437	4,581	4,632	4,411	4,643	4,591	4,481
MEATH	5,473	5,697	5,529	5,573	5,507	5,009	5,095	4,991	4,763
CAVAN	1,153	1,248	1,225	1,324	1,366	1,126	1,170	1,289	1,338
LOUTH	3,610	3,577	3,387	3,502	3,779	3,679	3,697	3,816	3,692
MONAGHAN	1,252	2,091	2,049	2,086	2,016	1,812	1,613	1,731	1,709
LAOIS	2,017	2,189	2,107	2,066	1,709	1,743	1,762	1,818	1,878
LONGFORD	1,005	1,017	1,026	1,050	1,037	0,895	0,922	1,007	1,091
OFFALY	2,034	2,149	2,065	2,071	1,970	1,779	1,895	1,952	2,057
ROSCOMMON	1,584	1,881	1,952	1,935	1,716	1,136	1,141	1,208	1,359
WESTMEATH	2,044	2,175	2,299	2,231	2,461	2,148	2,338	2,391	2,451

REGIONS	AGED 0-4	AGED 5-9	AGED 10-14	AGED 15-19	AGED 20-24	AGED 25-29	AGED 30-34	AGED 35-39	AGED 40-44
DONEGAL	5,188	5,645	5,568	5,592	5,694	4,914	4,698	4,703	4,503
NORTHWEST	2,287	2,545	2,606	2,682	2,672	2,256	2,407	2,549	2,758
WEST	8,762	9,626	9,907	10,277	10,648	8,852	9,231	9,669	10,096
MIDWEST	10,818	11,007	10,871	11,230	11,755	10,722	11,341	11,537	11,491
SOUTHWEST	17,730	18,392	18,011	18,499	18,489	17,932	18,561	19,363	19,967
SOUTHEAST	13,662	14,234	13,896	14,127	13,985	12,957	13,175	13,712	14,108
EAST	57,509	56,924	54,466	57,921	62,253	59,234	61,118	61,290	65,991
NORTHEAST	6,715	6,916	6,661	6,812	7,161	6,617	6,480	6,836	6,739
MIDLANDS	8,684	9,411	9,359	9,353	9,177	7,703	8,058	8,466	8,836

STATE	AGED 0-4	AGED 5-9	AGED 10-14	AGED 15-19	AGED 20-24	AGED 25-29	AGED 30-34	AGED 35-39	AGED 40-44
STATE	131,555	134,860	131,345	136,493	142,654	131,182	134,121	138,134	144,889

127

FEMALES 2006 CONTINUED

COUNTIES	AGED 45-49	AGED 50-54	AGED 55-59	AGED 60-64	AGED 65-69	AGED 70-74	AGED 75-79	AGED 80+	ALL AGES
DONEGAL	3,993	4,145	3,937	3,024	2,574	2,011	1,738	2,234	70,161
LEITRIM	683	811	688	526	499	447	380	476	9,688
SLIGO	2,043	2,010	1,765	1,300	1,141	927	837	1,099	28,726
GALWAY	6,683	6,251	5,434	4,167	3,450	2,895	2,383	2,904	92,574
MAYO	3,928	3,660	3,217	2,398	2,174	1,887	1,650	2,262	49,307
CLARE	3,092	3,232	3,144	2,260	1,805	1,386	1,149	1,392	49,432
LIMERICK – BOR	1,856	1,370	1,325	1,175	1,095	965	776	848	25,618
LIMERICK – CO	4,171	4,167	3,619	2,791	2,064	1,568	1,218	1,534	58,634
TIPPERARY – NR	1,705	1,776	1,618	1,350	1,049	1,000	823	1,017	26,039
CORK – BOR	1,624	2,762	2,875	2,746	2,096	2,433	1,949	2,298	58,082
CORK – CO	10,296	10,618	9,276	7,032	5,336	4,401	3,499	4,309	152,808
KERRY	3,729	3,955	3,631	2,792	2,360	1,992	1,685	2,113	56,477
CARLOW	1,612	1,361	1,203	964	758	640	499	593	20,858
KILKENNY	2,702	2,674	2,230	1,804	1,400	1,172	918	1,074	39,770
TIPPERARY – SR	2,359	2,395	2,191	1,612	1,373	1,135	987	1,223	35,307
WATERFORD – BOR	1,574	1,202	1,231	1,067	943	753	554	633	24,160
WATERFORD – CO	1,522	1,706	1,447	1,194	1,010	810	570	729	23,888
WEXFORD	3,369	3,260	3,031	2,526	1,999	1,647	1,322	1,623	50,388
DUBLIN – BOR	13,944	5,176	5,377	7,710	8,645	8,397	7,470	9,224	116,193
DUN LAOIRE	9,972	1,229	1,265	1,324	1,323	1,182	995	1,391	24,241
DUBLIN – CO	30,172	28,420	22,358	15,802	11,853	7,920	5,412	5,291	456,267
KILDARE	5,807	5,581	4,648	3,163	2,131	1,494	1,076	1,234	81,165
WICKLOW	4,208	4,008	3,622	2,750	2,010	1,554	1,259	1,505	61,791
MEATH	4,438	4,450	3,754	2,703	2,000	1,550	1,135	1,298	69,145
CAVAN	1,387	1,515	1,355	1,003	890	843	668	874	19,674
LOUTH	3,424	2,859	2,779	2,265	1,802	1,454	1,169	1,484	49,982
MONAGHAN	1,685	1,653	1,481	1,070	908	784	637	765	26,047
LAOIS	1,746	1,721	1,382	1,132	905	805	679	761	26,720
LONGFORD	1,044	1,054	963	714	550	503	452	531	14,951
OFFALY	1,796	1,839	1,666	1,311	1,041	898	728	609	28,700
ROSCOMMON	1,357	1,569	1,425	1,112	993	936	808	978	23,074
WESTMEATH	2,202	2,261	1,942	1,458	1,207	996	818	932	32,364

REGIONS	AGED 45-49	AGED 50-54	AGED 55-59	AGED 60-64	AGED 65-69	AGED 70-74	AGED 75-79	AGED 80+	ALL AGES
DONEGAL	3,993	4,145	3,937	3,024	2,574	2,011	1,738	2,234	70,161
NORTHWEST	2,726	2,821	2,453	1,826	1,640	1,374	1,217	1,575	38,414
WEST	9,712	9,920	8,651	6,565	5,624	4,782	4,033	5,256	141,881
MIDWEST	10,821	10,605	9,706	7,585	6,013	4,919	3,966	4,791	159,723
SOUTHWEST	18,559	17,335	15,782	12,575	10,502	8,826	7,133	8,720	267,367
SOUTHEAST	13,138	12,599	11,333	9,167	7,302	6,166	4,850	5,875	194,371
EAST	60,521	48,873	43,024	33,581	27,771	22,097	17,347	19,873	800,802
NORTHEAST	6,496	6,427	5,615	4,338	3,607	3,081	2,474	3,173	95,698
MIDLANDS	8,225	8,447	7,378	5,734	4,724	4,138	3,505	4,111	125,300

STATE	AGED 45-49	AGED 50-54	AGED 55-59	AGED 60-64	AGED 65-69	AGED 70-74	AGED 75-79	AGED 80+	ALL AGES
STATE	134,185	120,772	107,879	84,395	69,847	57,394	46,263	55,558	1,901,726

PERSONS 2006 CONTINUED

COUNTIES	AGED 0-4	AGED 5-9	AGED 10-14	AGED 15-19	AGED 20-24	AGED 25-29	AGED 30-34	AGED 35-39	AGED 40-44
DONEGAL	10,642	11,449	11,292	11,411	11,617	10,149	9,690	9,812	9,294
LEITRIM	1,101	1,279	1,314	1,326	1,473	1,062	1,080	1,163	1,354
SLIGO	3,722	4,030	4,105	4,271	4,212	3,602	3,745	4,017	4,245
GALWAY	12,232	12,805	12,900	13,659	14,370	12,798	12,741	13,560	14,167
MAYO	6,306	7,220	7,491	7,600	7,653	5,616	5,741	6,191	6,535
CLARE	7,484	7,873	7,729	7,853	7,877	5,139	7,399	7,237	6,968
LIMERICK – BOR	3,465	3,327	3,192	3,599	3,913	3,139	3,547	3,964	4,661
LIMERICK – CO	8,102	9,318	8,080	8,364	8,754	8,774	9,210	9,050	8,997
TIPPERARY – NR	3,276	3,331	3,271	3,304	3,772	3,563	3,698	3,823	3,981
CORK – BOR	5,321	7,162	6,792	7,308	8,254	7,406	8,022	9,441	11,019
CORK – CO	21,321	22,811	22,193	22,676	23,792	22,860	23,360	23,287	22,715
KERRY	7,401	8,046	7,730	8,415	8,739	7,645	7,805	7,932	8,204
CARLOW	2,894	3,025	2,907	2,849	3,156	3,028	3,207	3,208	3,363
KILKENNY	6,022	6,445	6,363	6,463	6,112	5,559	5,515	5,660	5,671
TIPPERARY – SR	5,158	5,480	5,507	5,808	5,703	5,069	5,069	5,319	5,802
WATERFORD – BOR	3,736	3,829	3,728	3,047	3,780	3,330	3,325	3,547	3,556
WATERFORD – CO	3,205	3,461	3,335	3,302	3,477	3,589	3,498	3,654	3,686
WEXFORD	7,173	7,304	7,049	7,130	7,715	7,204	7,417	7,700	7,532
DUBLIN – BOR	5,146	9,503	9,098	4,224	14,303	11,158	10,115	15,232	27,137
DUN LAOIRE	2,613	2,414	2,349	2,771	3,378	2,570	2,570	3,193	4,107
DUBLIN – CO	77,342	80,523	76,911	76,659	71,803	71,200	73,372	71,192	66,134
KILDARE	13,113	13,047	12,625	13,083	12,771	12,071	13,779	13,170	12,756
WICKLOW	9,264	9,389	9,051	9,249	9,325	8,882	9,346	9,048	8,849
MEATH	11,272	11,761	11,411	11,503	11,671	10,535	10,567	10,376	9,045
CAVAN	2,434	2,625	2,677	2,725	3,111	2,607	2,709	2,879	3,136
LOUTH	7,504	7,422	7,011	7,213	7,600	7,302	7,313	7,525	7,384
MONAGHAN	4,037	4,334	4,246	4,386	4,366	4,008	3,595	4,047	4,103
LAOIS	4,207	4,546	4,132	4,481	4,491	3,927	3,780	4,212	4,103
LONGFORD	2,036	2,113	2,121	2,201	2,261	2,030	2,030	2,212	2,276
OFFALY	4,266	4,501	4,347	4,448	4,306	3,941	4,104	4,179	4,469
ROSCOMMON	3,240	3,839	3,085	3,093	3,653	2,696	2,563	2,917	2,969
WESTMEATH	4,273	4,467	4,490	4,671	5,061	4,497	4,730	5,057	5,222

REGIONS	AGED 0-4	AGED 5-9	AGED 10-14	AGED 15-19	AGED 20-24	AGED 25-29	AGED 30-34	AGED 35-39	AGED 40-44
DONEGAL	10,642	11,449	11,292	11,411	11,617	10,149	9,690	9,812	9,294
NORTHWEST	4,821	5,309	5,419	5,597	5,685	4,664	4,825	5,180	5,599
WEST	18,508	20,025	20,391	21,259	22,032	18,414	18,820	19,760	20,702
MIDWEST	22,266	22,849	22,272	23,120	24,316	22,597	23,854	24,074	24,607
SOUTHWEST	36,508	38,000	37,062	38,399	40,775	37,911	39,187	40,660	41,938
SOUTHEAST	28,278	29,444	28,772	29,679	30,233	27,618	28,031	29,093	29,610
EAST	118,950	117,697	112,249	117,579	124,101	117,248	119,749	122,211	128,928
NORTHEAST	13,975	14,381	13,884	14,324	15,167	14,007	13,617	14,044	14,265
MIDLANDS	18,022	19,456	19,382	19,794	19,852	17,086	17,207	18,407	19,039

	AGED 0-4	AGED 5-9	AGED 10-14	AGED 15-19	AGED 20-24	AGED 25-29	AGED 30-34	AGED 35-39	AGED 40-44
STATE	272,060	278,579	270,723	281,162	293,868	269,694	274,980	283,241	293,982

129

COUNTIES	AGED 45-49	AGED 50-54	AGED 55-59	AGED 60-64	AGED 65-69	AGED 70-74	AGED 75-79	AGED 80+	ALL AGES
DONEGAL	8,219	8,546	8,035	6,399	5,204	4,010	3,194	3,598	142,561
LEITRIM*	1,442	1,565	1,418	1,091	1,033	894	720	777	20,082
SLIGO	4,009	3,989	3,620	2,621	2,215	1,774	1,472	1,619	57,266
GALWAY	13,203	12,438	11,044	8,456	6,663	5,526	4,188	4,677	186,143
MAYO	6,608	6,564	6,860	5,188	4,457	3,830	3,064	3,564	121,488
CLARE	6,587	6,600	6,313	4,598	3,639	2,699	2,061	2,702	102,240
LIMERICK – BOR	3,980	2,812	2,664	2,218	2,060	1,674	1,222	1,168	50,513
LIMERICK – CO	8,623	8,522	7,347	5,580	4,125	3,007	2,102	2,248	119,218
TIPPERARY – NR	3,618	3,491	3,213	2,543	2,022	1,818	1,307	1,307	51,588
CORK – BOR	5,429	5,787	5,512	5,133	5,050	4,133	3,007	3,039	113,749
CORK – CO	21,126	21,174	18,588	13,777	10,488	8,077	5,964	6,244	311,158
KERRY	7,906	7,781	7,191	5,026	4,831	3,888	2,999	3,308	116,697
CARLOW	3,171	2,781	2,402	1,969	1,463	1,136	1,584	841	41,930
KILKENNY	5,530	5,296	4,548	3,550	2,710	2,129	1,654	1,633	80,990
TIPPERARY – SR	5,068	5,008	4,414	3,252	2,684	2,093	1,654	1,797	74,904
WATERFORD – BOR	2,938	2,411	2,327	2,031	1,750	1,350	882	874	47,353
WATERFORD – CO	3,191	3,337	2,946	2,327	1,837	1,403	1,013	801	48,625
WEXFORD	6,979	6,572	6,014	4,948	3,999	3,028	2,279	2,431	102,465
DUBLIN – BOR	26,195	25,808	13,303	14,135	15,277	14,020	11,476	12,288	204,513
DUN LAOIRE	3,543	2,348	2,292	2,266	2,198	1,882	1,483	1,695	43,594
DUBLIN – CO	58,709	55,172	43,779	20,360	21,490	13,882	8,615	7,405	904,157
KILDARE	11,852	11,116	9,333	6,380	4,125	2,739	1,813	1,812	167,335
WICKLOW	8,277	7,811	7,139	5,334	3,917	2,856	2,036	2,170	121,943
MEATH	9,066	8,847	7,685	5,626	3,804	2,793	1,949	1,962	140,953
CAVAN	3,142	3,122	2,788	2,107	1,790	1,611	1,269	1,337	42,109
LOUTH	6,722	5,840	5,184	4,376	3,435	2,573	1,857	2,119	98,670
MONAGHAN	3,521	3,370	2,994	2,170	1,730	1,471	1,142	1,179	53,934
LAOIS	3,683	3,473	2,800	2,275	1,800	1,454	1,170	1,207	55,883
LONGFORD	2,116	2,177	1,954	1,492	1,122	976	736	787	30,550
OFFALY	3,870	3,658	3,241	2,563	2,100	1,691	1,288	1,403	58,464
ROSCOMMON	3,022	3,315	2,886	2,307	2,011	1,837	1,489	1,557	48,274
WESTMEATH	4,726	4,555	3,913	2,910	2,318	1,821	1,411	1,414	65,531

REGIONS	AGED 45-49	AGED 50-54	AGED 55-59	AGED 60-64	AGED 65-69	AGED 70-74	AGED 75-79	AGED 80+	ALL AGES
DONEGAL	8,219	8,546	8,035	6,399	5,204	4,010	3,194	3,598	142,561
NORTHWEST	5,451	5,554	5,038	3,702	3,248	2,668	2,192	2,396	77,348
WEST	19,301	20,002	17,904	13,644	11,420	9,356	7,252	8,241	287,631
MIDWEST	22,808	21,432	19,537	14,047	11,854	9,198	6,782	7,146	323,659
SOUTHWEST	38,520	34,073	31,591	24,736	20,360	16,098	11,970	12,793	541,604
SOUTHEAST	26,882	25,408	22,651	17,076	14,449	11,229	8,242	8,665	396,267
EAST	117,542	95,103	83,531	63,710	50,891	38,172	27,372	27,372	1,582,495
NORTHEAST	13,585	12,332	11,166	8,653	6,955	5,655	4,268	4,635	194,713
MIDLANDS	17,426	17,178	14,794	11,457	9,351	7,779	6,094	6,368	258,702
STATE	270,241	240,533	214,247	165,224	133,741	104,165	77,366	81,174	3,804,980

APPENDIX 3

Projections of Number of Elderly Persons Living Alone, 1981 — 2006 (Prepared for the National Council for the Aged by John Blackwell)

Trends 1ᐤ71-81

Before the projections are given, the main trends in the number of persons aged 65 and over who are living alone can be given. Table 1 gives the trends for those living in permanent housing units. As there is little information available on the number of persons by age and sex who were living in temporary housing units in 1971, the trends over 1971-81 are given for those who live in permanent housing units only. The marked increase in the number of elderly persons living alone between 1971 and 1981 can be noted, as well as the differences in the trends for males and for females.

There was a substantial increase in the number of elderly persons living alone in temporary housing units between 1971 and 1981: from 269 in 1971 to 1949 in 1981. Of the 1949 elderly persons living alone in temporary housing units in 1981, 1231 were males and 718 were females. Table 2 gives an age and sex breakdown for the elderly persons living in temporary housing units in 1ᐤ81. This table also gives the resulting number of elderly persons living alone in all types of housing units, both permanent and temporary.

Projections to 2006: the method

The projections of the number of elderly persons living alone are done for the age groups 65 and over and 75 and over respectively, for those living in permanent housing units and in temporary housing units respectively, and by sex. First, a brief outline of the method is given.

The method is based on projecting the number of elderly persons who are either single or widowed, by sex. These projections are done as follows. The assumptions about the proportion of women aged 65 and over who are married in 1986 and 1991 are the same as in the CSO projections of April 1985.[1] For the subsequent period, the proportions married are held at their 1991 values. The assumptions are outlined in Table 3.

131

It is assumed that the ratio of married males aged 65 and over to married females aged 65 and over is 1.60 throughout the projection period: the corresponding ratio was 1.64 in 1971 and 1.59 in 1981.

The other main element which drives the projections is the assumption about the ratio of independent households of the elderly to the number of single and widowed elderly persons. The key ratio is the ratio of the number of one person households to the number of persons who are either single or widowed. The trends in this ratio over the decade 1971-1981 show a considerable increase in the propensity of elderly persons to form independent household and to live alone rather than live in households with other persons such as in-laws. The ratios are as follows, for those living in permanent housing units.

	1971	1981
males	24.6%	32.4%
females	20.4%	30.6%

For the period up to 2006 the assumed ratios are derived by a modified linear extrapolation, that is, it is assumed that the average annual change (in percentage point terms) is half of the period 1971-1981.

For those who live in temporary housing units, there is (as indicated above) less information on the 1971 position. Hence, a formal extrapolation of household formation rates is not used. Rather, account is taken of the trends over 1971-81 in the number of all elderly persons (both male and female) who live alone in temporary housing units and account is taken of the projected number of elderly persons.

For those aged 75 and over, assumptions are made about the proportion of women who are ever-married, up to 1996, and the ratio of those married to those ever-married of 1981 is then applied. The resulting proportion of women who are married of 1996 is held constant for the remainder of the projection period. The assumptions are outlined in Table 3. In other respects, the method used for those aged 75 and over is the same as that outlined for those aged 65 and over. It is assumed that the ratio of married males to married females is 2.10 throughout the projection period: this was the ratio in 1981. The equivalent household formation rates are as follows, again for those who live in permanent housing units.

	1971	1981
males	19.9%	27.7%
females	16.7%	25.8%

Once again, the distinct rise in the rates of household formation between 1971 and 1981 can be observed.

132

Results of the projections

The results of the projections are given in Table 4.

(1) *Population and Labour Force Projections, 1986-1991,* Central Statistics Office, Dublin, 1985.

Table 1: *Number of Elderly Persons living alone in permanent housing units, 1971 and 1981*

Age	1971	1981	% change 1971-81
	Males	Males	
65-69	5,895	8,268	+ 40.3
70-74	5,280	6,900	+ 30.7
75 and over	5,587	7,654	+ 37.0
65 and over	16,762	22,822	+36.2
	Females	Females	
65-69	7,958	12,844	+61.4
70-74	8,936	12,958	+45.0
75 and over	9,453	17,461	+84.7
65 and over	26,347	43,263	+64.2

Source: *Census of Population, 1981, Volume 3,* Central Statistics Office, Dublin.

133

Table 2: *Number of Elderly Persons living alone in temporary housing units and in all housing units by age and sex in 1981*

Age	Males	Females
	In temporary housing unts	
65-59	466	190
70-74	390	238
75 and over	375	290
65 and over	1,231	718
	In all housing units	
65-69	8,734	13,034
70-74	7,290	13,196
75 and over	8,029	17,751
65 and over	24,053	43,981

Source: *Census of Population 1981, V olume 3,* Central Statistics Office, Dublin.

Table 3: *Assumptions on proportion of Elderly Women married, 1986-2006*

Year	Aged 65 and over %	Aged 75 and over %
1981 (actual)	29.3	14.9
1986	32.0	15.2
1991	33.0	15.3
1996	33.0	15.4
2001	33.0	15.4
2006	33.0	15.4

Table 4: *Projections of Elderly Persons living alone, 1981-2006*

Year	In permanent housing units	In temporary housing units	Thousands In all housing units
Males aged 65 and over			
1981 (actual)	22.8	1.2	24.1
1986	20.0	1.5	21.5
1991	18.4	1.6	20.0
1996	18.2	1.7	19.9
2001	18.3	1.8	20.1
2006	19.6	1.9	21.5
Females aged 65 and over			
1981 (actual)	43.3	0.7	44.0
1986	48.2	0.9	49.1
1991	52.8	1.0	53.8
1996	57.0	1.1	58.1
2001	60.9	1.2	62.1
2006	66.6	1.3	67.9
Males aged 75 and over			
1981 (actual)	7.7	0.4	8.0
1986	8.6	0.45	9.05
1991	9.3	0.5	9.8
1996	9.3	0.55	9.85
2001	9.1	0.6	9.7
2006	8.9	0.65	9.55
Females aged 75 and over			
1981 (actual)	17.5	0.3	17.8
1986	20.1	0.35	20.45
1991	23.6	0.4	24.0
1996	26.4	0.45	26.85
2001	29.5	0.5	30.0
2006	32.0	0.55	32.55

APPENDIX 4

Exceptional compassionate grounds for allocation of housing points by Dublin Corporation

Introduction
Most housing cases have an element of compassion in them. When considering cases under the category of Exceptional Compassionate Grounds, therefore, the emphasis must be on the exceptional nature of the application. A definition of Exceptional could be:

"Any unusual factor or circumstances related to housing which is having a grave effect on the applicant(s) and which is not already taken into consideration within the points system".

Procedure
The Chief Welfare Officer and one of his assistants examine each request submitted for consideration on Exceptional Compassionate Grounds. When necessary, the housing file is requested and further details are gathered. A decision to recommend points or overall priority is determined by three considerations:

(a) *If the circumstances are truly exceptional:*

Most people see their housing needs as exceptional. An overview of the social climate in Dublin is necessary, however, to determine what is and what is not exceptional. Exceptional circumstances can also become common over a period of years, in a rapidly changing society. For example drug abuse was seen as exceptional some years ago. Tragically it can no longer be considered as such;

(b) *If the circumstances are not already taken into consideration in the points system:*

Representations are often made for points on Exceptional Compassionate Grounds in cases which are medical. Sometimes medical points have been awarded, and there is a false expectation that the required extra points

136

can be obtained on Exceptional Compassionate Grounds. Points or overall priority cannot be recommended in circumstances which are medical only, or in cases of normal overcrowding;

(c) *If overall priority or points are necessary in cases which are exceptional, to resolve the housing needs of the applicants:*

For example, some people live in deplorable circumstances and in situations which are truly exceptional. However, they are prepared to continue living in such conditions and to even put their children in moral or physical danger in order to get the accommodation *they* want – which is often a house in a high priority area.

Housing Stock:

A favourable recommendation on Exceptional Compassionate Grounds means that somebody moves up the housing priority list and others as a result move down. Points or overall priority are recommended, therefore, with this in view. Recommendations of extra points or overall priority are also more easily made in cases where the applicant is prepared to move to low demand accommodation, or to similar type accommodation.

During 1982, some 1,600 cases were considered on Exceptional Compassionate Grounds. 90 cases were recommended for overall priority and 60 for points. Delays in processing cases on Exceptional Compassionate Grounds are principally due to the length of time required to get reports. However, in cases of extreme urgency, a referral on Exceptional Compassionate Grounds can be processed in a matter of hours if the appropriate information is available.

Source: Kelly, M.A., Chief Welfare Officer, Dublin Corporation.

137

APPENDIX 5
Diagrammatic Representation of Community Context for Sheltered Housing Schemes.

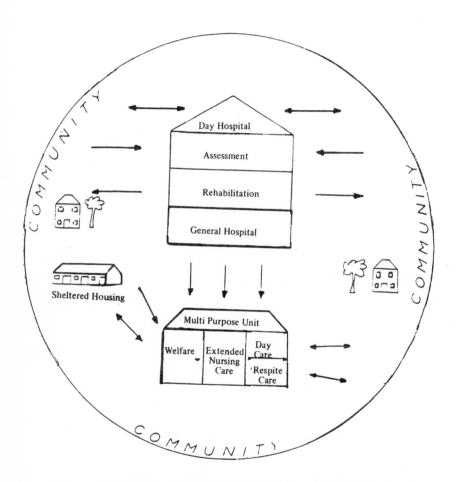

Source: *Institutional Geriatric Care in Eastern Health Board Area, Medium Term Programme for Capital Development,* Eastern Health Board, 1984

Appendix 6

LEGISLATION RELEVANT TO VOLUNTARY HOUSING ASSOCIATIONS

HOUSING ACT, 1966.

Assistance by housing authority of certain bodies.
12. (1) A housing authority may, with the consent of the Minister and on such terms and conditions as they think fit, assist another housing authority or a body to which this section applies, either in respect of the provision by the other authority or by the body of housing accommodation or in respect of some other matter, in one or more of the following ways:

(a) by a loan

(b) by a periodic contribution to the funds of the other authority or the body.

(c) by a guarantee of the sums owned by the other authority or by the body in respect of borrowings.

(2) This section applies to the following bodies:

(a) a body whose objects include at least one of the following:

(i) the provision of dwellings for elderly persons,

(ii) the provision of dwellings which will help to secure one or more of the primary objectives to which a housing authority are required by sub-section (3) of this section 60 of this Act to have regard.

(iii) the advance of money for the provision (including reconstruction or purchase) of dwellings,

(iv) the conduct in relation to housing of research or the provision of training,

(b) any other body approved by the Minister for the purposes of this section.

(3) A guarantee under this section may be given by the housing authority either alone or jointly with any other person or persons.

(4) A decision of making a periodic contribution or to give a loan or guarantee under this section shall be a reserved function.

HOUSING (MISC. PROVISIONS) ACT, 1979

Grants by Minister for expenses of certain bodies.
3. (1) The Minister may, with the consent of the Minister for Finance, pay, out of moneys provided by the Oireachtas, a grant in respect of the administrative and general expenses of a body to which this section applies and which is approved of by the Minister for the purposes of this section.

(2) This section applies to a body which represents or promotes the formation of co-operative groups or voluntary associations which have as an object the provision of houses.

(3) A grant under this section shall be subject to such terms and conditions as may be determined by the Minister at the time of the making of the grant.

(4) This section shall be deemed to have come into operation on the 1st day of January, 1979.

Appendix 7

LEGAL INCORPORATION FOR VOLUNTARY HOUSING ASSOCIATIONS

Legal Incorporation
Voluntary, caring and self-help co-operative housing associations can obtain legal incorporation with limited liability status.

The method most commonly used by the voluntary housing groups caring for the elderly or other disadvantaged categories who wish to legally incorporate is to register under the Companies Act.

This involves the adoption of a Memorandum and Articles of Association (i.e. a constitution and rules) for a non-profit company *limited by guarantee and not having share capital.* This type of company is widely used by voluntary bodies who wish to achieve legal incorporation.

The Memorandum lists the aims or objects of the Association and defines its non-profit, philanthropic or caring intentions.

The Articles are largely based on the requirements of the Companies Acts relating to the proper management of a company formed without sharehold, including provisions for membership, meetings, board of directors or executive committee, officers, contracts, accounts and auditing etc.

Charitable Status
Voluntary housing and other types of caring associations sometimes refer to themselves as 'charities' but this is not strictly speaking correct, although they do have bona fide philanthropic purposes aiming at the relief of deprivation and operate for the benefit of the community.

The term *Charity* in its legal sense applies to a scheme approved by the

141

Commissioners of Charitable Donations and Bequests for which trustees are appointed as a body corporate subject to the supervision and control of the Commissioners under the Charities Acts 1961 and 1973.

However, provided the Memorandum and Articles of Association adopted by a voluntary housing group under the Companies Act meet the requirements of the Revenue Commissioners as regards non-profit philanthropic purposes relating to relief of deprivation and poverty, advancement of education and research and purposes beneficial to the community the association can be granted exemption from tax.

Such exemption is only granted on an individual basis so each group has to apply separately to the Claims Branch, Revenue Commissioners, 19 Dame Street, Dublin. Exemption from rates is a separate matter requiring application to the local authority in the first instance and then the Commissioner of Valuation. Housing units are not liable to rates.

The model Memorandum and Articles published by The Housing Centre are approved by the Revenue Commissioners for non-profit companies with charitable purposes seeking tax exemption.

A procedure also exists to omit the word *Limited* from the title name of the company/association. This involves application to the Minister for Trade, Commerce and Tourism to issue a licence permitting the registration of the company without the word limited as usually required by the Companies Act. This procedure is carried out at the time of the formation of the company and the licence is submitted to the Registrar of Companies.

Model Memorandum and Articles of Association for a Voluntary Housing Association
The Housing Centre provides a model Memorandum and Articles of Association for registration of a housing association as a non-profit company limited by guarantee and not having share capital.

Source: The Housing Centre, Dublin.

Appendix 8

THE GUIDING PRINCIPLES OF THE ABBEYFIELD SOCIETY

The Abbeyfield Society, founded as an expression of Christian concern for the elderly, is a co-operative effort by people of faith and goodwill.

Members of the Abbeyfield Society believe:

> that elderly people have an important role to play amongst their families, friends and community;

> that many elderly people suffer from loneliness and insecurity;

> that within the community the individual has an essential part ot play in helping elderly people in special need.

The Society's purpose, therefore, is to provide the elderly with their own homes within the security and companionship of small households, which can become focal points for goodwill and friendly contact within the community.

The following pattern has been evolved to achieve this purpose:

> In all areas wherever there is a need a local Abbeyfield Society is set up which will have full local responsibility for opening and maintaining Abbeyfield houses.

> Houses are situated in the communities from which the residents are usually drawn.

> Loneliness is the primary consideration in the selection of residents.

> Residents have rooms of their own, furnish them as they wish and look after them.

> The privacy of each resident's room is respected, but visits from relations, friends and neighbours are encouraged.

Each resident pays his or her share of the full running costs of the house.

A housekeeper residing in each house cares for the residents, runs the house and provides and prepares the main meals.

Local clergy and ministers are made aware of the house and given the opportunity to visit as in an ordinary home. Any arrangements for services or prayers within the house are made in accordance with the wishes of the residents.

In sharing these beliefs, and following this general pattern of work, local Societies achieve the purpose of the Abbeyfield Society.

The Volunteers

Abbeyfield Societies are voluntary-work organisations: the only paid members of staff are the housekeepers and their reliefs.

This statement is braodly true of the whole Abbeyfield movement, although in certain circumstances it is possible for small honoraria to tbe paid. With the increasing administration of a local Society with several houses, it has been found in a few cases that some forms of administrative work can be handled more economically and efficiently on a paid basis. But these cases are still a small minority.

Volunteers, therefore, are the life blood of a local Society. A properly constituted Executive Committee will have among its members a solicitor, to deal with legal matters, a bank manager or accountant, to deal with financial affairs, a builder or surveyor, to advise on property matters and a doctor to advise on medical matters and liaise with the medical profession. It will have elected a Chairman and a Treasurer, and will need to appoint an Hon. Secretary whose duties will include servicing the Executive Committee meetings and co-ordinating the work of the members.

In addition, it is desirable to appoint on Organising/Applications Secretary, to be responsible for the day-to-day administration of the Society's houses, including selection of residents, dealing with enquiries, and liaison between the housekeepers, the houses and the Committee.

Except in the case of one-house Societies, it is usual to have a House Committee of two or three members, chaired by a member of the Executive Committee, for each house. Each member takes a particular responsibility, e.g. for collecting residents' payments, for maintenance of the house and

144

garden, for keeping a tactful eye on the housekeeping expenditure and assisting with bulk buying.

A wise Society, given a volunteer with suitable interest and expertise, will appoint a Committee member to take responsibility for relations with the press and with other bodies working with elderly people in the area, and for generally publicising the work of the Society.

Besides these voluntary Committee members, whose responsibilities require fairly specific amounts of time, a successful Society will develop a network of helpers among those whose time cannot be given on such a regular basis. Their contributions may take the form of occasionally taking a resident shopping or to church; working in the garden; helping to organise coffee mornings and the like; typing correspondence; preparing meals for the residents on the housekeeper's day off, and generally assisting in the houshold in times of stress.

THE ABBEYFIELD (DUBLIN) SOCIETY LIMITED.
Correspondence Secretary:
Mrs. Caroline Kennedy,
Avon Cottage,
Foxrock, Dublin 18.

Appendix 9

LEASEHOLD SCHEMES FOR THE ELDERLY IN GREAT BRITAIN

1.1 Nearly twenty years ago, a housing association in Surrey completed a scheme for the elderly to which the tenants, by taking up loan stock, contributed part of the capital cost, the balance being funded by a local authority loan. During the sixties, other associations developed various schemes which combined investment by the occupants with finance from public sources.

1.2 It was in the early seventies that the first known sheltered housing scheme was launched which was financed entirely by the tenants. They occupied their homes under normal tenancy agreements and made their investment by way of loan stock issued by the association. Since then, this pioneering spirit has been echoed by other associations who have experimented with other forms of tenure.

1.3 Most of the early schemes provided only for repayment of the original capital contribution but, with the surge in property values, prospective tenants began to question the prudence of re-investing the whole or greater part of their capital in property without also participating in any equity appreciation. Simultaneously it became evident that, as development costs rose, many elderly owner occupiers lived in properties which would not realise enough capital for them to invest in this type of housing association scheme.

1.4 The National Dwelling and Housing Survey published in 1978 identifies 2.1 million elderly owner occupiers and, in common with other population trends, this number is expected to rise over the next two decades. Even if only 5% of the number seek sheltered accommodation, then there is a clear measure of an urgent demand. The speculative developer has recognised the potential market and in some degree is catering for a part of the need. But

146

the voluntary housing movement has its own relevant specialist skills, a long standing tradition of complementing the housing provision made by others, and the potential to make a significant contribution to meeting this particular challenge.

1.5 By drawing upon the experience of all of its members who had engaged in the early innovative schemes, the National Federation of Housing Associations has devised the new arrangements called Leasehold Schemes for the Elderly. These are sponsored by the Department of the Environment and the Housing Corporation, and form part of a pilot programme of equity sharing schemes which are partially funded by housing association grant.

What the new scheme is all about
1.6 Leasehold Schemes for the Elderly are intended to provide choice for elderly owner occupiers of limited income, many of whom have virtually all their capital tied up in the modest property which is their home. For those who would like to move into accommodation more suitable for their needs, there may be no effective choice at present. There is unlikely to be smaller, more convenient accommodation in their home locality, or nearer friends and relations, at a price they can afford; much of the property built privately for retirement is sited far from shops and local centres of activity; the private sector does not provide sheltered housing with the security to the elderly of having someone on hand in case of emergency. Elderly owner occupiers are often precluded from obtaining local authority rented housing on the grounds that they are 'adequately housed' or 'have too much capital'. Even for housing association property, they may also have a low priority.

1.7 Yet to the occupier, the capital asset of the house is of little value unless it is sold: and many on low or fixed incomes can suffer acute hardship despite their status as owner occupiers. Leasehold Schemes for the Elderly offer fulfilment of a real housing need. The community also benefits by the retention of private investment in housing; reduction of cost of care later in life; and, in many cases, the release of under-occupied property on to the market for family occupation.

The people who will be helped
1.8 The prospective leaseholders will probably be in their seventies or even older, with an occasional 60-70 year old. The majority will be on their own but there will be some married couples and some households of friends or relatives sharing. They will be finding their present home too large, too inconvenient, and too expensive to maintain and the garden a worry. Their house may be rather isolated from its neighbours or the locality may have

147

changed in character in recent years so that they no longer feel at home. Relatively few will have generous occupational pensions and inflation will be making it increasingly hard to manage on what they have. Some may be in receipt of supplementary benefit. Any surplus from the sale of their present home, after re-investing in a leasehold scheme, will also help towards their financial independence and maintanenace of a reasonable standard of living. The amount of capital they will have for investment in a scheme will vary with the value of the property they have to put on the market, the level of their savings, and any contributions from other sources, perhaps from younger relatives or from converted pension rights. A few may not even be owner occupiers but have adequate capital resources.

How the scheme works
1.9 The scheme devised is as simple as is consistent with reconciling the different interests of the leaseholder, the landlord, and the taxpayer who provides the subsidy.

1.10 A 60 year lease provides a readily acceptable title to ownership effectively for the life of the leaseholder.

1.11 Housing Association Grant makes a contribution, generally 30% of the total costs, so that the price can be within the reach of owners of rather ordinary properties and a development can include warden's accommodation and some common facilities within the price.

1.12 Each property is bought and sold at 70% of value, which takes account of the contribution made by HAG. This principle achieves two objects: the leaseholders share in any equity appreciation; and succeeding occupants benefit from the reduction in price conferred by the public subsidy.

1.13 The lease reverts to the association at the end of the leaseholder's occupation. Thus the responsibility for granting a new lease to maintain the purpose of the government grant rests with an accountable body.

1.14 The total cost of each scheme is covered by the sum of the premiums paid for the lease plus HAG. During construction, the Housing Corporation will provide finance in the usual way, the bridging finance being repaid when all leases have been sold.

1.15 The assocation retains management responsibility for the scheme, including warden service, maintenance and repair, and maintaining a list of potential leaseholders.

An alternative

1.16 It is noticeable from the statistics that a large proportion of elderly people own properties built before 1919 which, in many cases, may be un-improved and of too low a value for them to participate in the basic Lease-hold Scheme for the Elderly. Especially with this group in mind, the Federation is turning its attention to developing an alternative financial framework which will involve a lower level of capital investment and which will also open up a wider choice to those with savings but no property to sell.

APPENDIX 10

FIRE SAFETY FOR THE ELDERLY AT HOME

What do older people need to know about fire?
It is vitally important to give people the information they need when they need it. People need different kinds of fire safety information depending on where they live, what they do, and how old they are. The following factors have been identified as vital in the fight to prevent older people being seriously injured or killed by fire.

(1) Older people are most frequently involved in fires between 7 and 10 a.m. It is believed that this is due to the fact that older people tend to be groggy when they rise and become increasingly alert as the day goes on. Early morning fire and burn accidents can be minimised by purchasing flame retardant sleepwear, not smoking in the early morning, being sure to turn off the gas between the first and second matches, and avoiding hazardous tasks until later in the day.

(2) Smoking is the number one cause of fire and burn deaths among older people. Specifically, the highest risk situation is one which can be called the fatal triangle. The triangle is comprised of a cigarette smoked in an over-stuffed chair by a person who is either tired or under stress and/or the influence of alcohol or drugs. Like the fire triangle, if one of these elements can be removed the risk is dramatically reduced.

(3) Young people are advised to stop, drop and roll if their clothes catch fire. Older people for whom falls are an ever greater hazard than fire, may find that this advice creates more problems than it solves. They should learn to remove burning clothes or wrap themselves in a blanket as quickly as possible.

(4) Prevention of clothing ignition is of prime importance. Older people

150

Are all plugs properly wired and fused?

Is care taken to avoid plugging more than one appliance at a time into a single socket source?

Is care taken to ensure that flexes never trail across hot or wet surfaces, and that appliances are never handled with wet hands?

Is care taken to ensure that portable mains-operated appliances are never used in the bathroom?

Is the electric kettle always unplugged before filling or pouring from it?

At bedtime are all appliances not in use during the night switched off and unplugged?

What to do in case of a fire

A plan of action should be prepared so that you will know exactly what to do in the event of a fire. The first priority is to get out, and once out – stay out. Do not go back for any reason.

1. Get out – plan safe escape routs (at least two) *now* – even if you never have to use them.

2. Do not delay in gathering possessions. If possible keep valuable documents in a box that you can quickly locate and take with you.

3. Do remember that in most cases it is the toxic fumes generated by fire that kill not flames themselves. If you are caught in smoke while leaving, let yourself down to the floor and crawl. Better air is near the floor.

4. Close doors and windows to reduce draughts which may fan the fire, (as long as you can do so without risk to yourself).

5. Have an arrangement (with neighbour?) for calling the fire brigade at once.

6. If you think you might be trapped by fire outside your room your pre-planning *now* for rescue is urgent. You should have a phone by your bed (if possible), a working flashlight and white cloth to signal at the window, and a cloth to stuff the cracks under the door. Your door must be closed to keep smoke out.

7. Plan now how you would escape in a fire emergency. Rehearse your fire escape plan and what to do if you become trapped.

Remember that people retain information best if they have a chance to see something and to practise it. Therefore have older people practise emergency escape plans, relighting pilot lights, switching off and unplugging appliances and other safety measures. A caring concerned attitude of mind is essential.

Source: *Costello, P.C., Chief Executive Officer of the Fire Prevention Council; Alert (Discontinued Newsletter of the Society of St. Vincent de Paul), November, 1982.*

156